cre·ate

verb \krē-ˈāt, ˈkrē\

a: To make or bring into existence something new
b: To produce through imaginative skill, design

Passion to Create

Passion to Create

YOUR INVITATION TO CELEBRATE

CHERYL CECCHETTO

NEW HOLLAND

"To be yourself in a world that is constantly trying to make you something else is the greatest accomplishment."
—Ralph Waldo Emerson

FOREWORD, HO

One sunny day in 1987, I was careening down Melrose Avenue in Hollywood, desperately trying to keep a late model, two-door Cadillac convertible from veering off the road. Flustered as I was, the Academy Award®-winning actress, Shelley Winters, relentlessly screaming from the backseat, "Let me drive!" was not helping. Shelley, in her late sixties, was still quite the tour-de-force in Hollywood, and not in the habit of taking a backseat to anyone.

"I want to drive! You work for ME!" she wailed. It was her car, after all, but I had my doubts whether or not Shelley had driven it since it went out of style in the early '70s. If she had, then I was convinced she had not driven it well. Eventually I surrendered, as it was really a toss up between which Shelley I wanted to deal with—an increasingly hysterical Shelley, or a Shelley behind the wheel. Once in the back seat, I longed for the hysterical Shelley as she meandered from left lane to right lane and back again on our way to her house in Beverly Hills. Driving her big boat of a car, she was only slightly less hysterical but at least she was happy. Now it was my turn to scream for my life, also for the sake of all the hapless pedestrians in Shelley's warpath whom I desperately waved out of the way. Through it all, some bewildered part of me watched from above and wondered, "How did I get here, and, besides to the emergency room at any moment, where am I going?"

I come from a big, loud, passionate, loud, small-town, loud Italian family. Our happy gatherings, heated debates, and epic arguments (and there were many), always centered around food, home-grown entertainment, arm-flailing exchanges, and hysterical laughter... all at the same time. They still do. Our gatherings were steeped in love, so much love. They still are.

As soon as I was old enough, I made myself indispensable in creating the countless skits, games, and musical performances at our many weddings, anniversaries, birthday parties, showers, you name it. I pulled everyone into the action to perform all the parts, with me usually "playing" mother, as well as playing my accordion wherever I could. (Don't laugh. I won awards.) It's true, I admit it: I love attention and always have. I constantly included everyone else as well, so that we could all be at the center of attention.

Many years later, I find myself in the thrilling—however unplanned—position of producing some of the most cutting edge events in Hollywood, the so-called "Entertainment Capital of the World". Hollywood's famous tagline puts any event producer to the test. Perhaps I should have seen this coming. My original joy of including everyone in celebration has evolved into a career of conceiving and creating singular environments that transcend time and space while reconnecting people in warm recognition of each other, their achievements, and their milestones. From lavish celebrations to intimate gatherings, I am determined to tempt everyone back to the table, eye-to-eye, ear-to-ear, toe-to-toe, pass the pasta, taste the wine, and how was your day?

At international speaking engagements, I am always asked three questions:

- How did you come to do what you do?
- Where do you get your ideas?
- What's going on in Hollywood?
- Oh, and a fourth question: "When are you going to write a book?"

What I do: My current career as an event producer is not what I had intended, but I have always opted for taking action. Originally, I wanted to be an actor and I studied the performing arts. That education and training informed my penchant for dramatic, dynamic, evolving events. My search for a survival job while I was a young actress living in Los Angeles drove me back to my roots. Eventually, this career chose me.

Ideas: Inspiration arrives from many places such as books, museums, movies, music, nature, travel, world events, and especially from friends and family. My mind is always buzzing. When ideas show up, I pay attention. It's amazing where your own ideas will take you when you simply roll up your sleeves and get to work.

The Hollywood scene: The film and television that Hollywood produces is the result of innumerable directors, writers, producers, actors, and many untold artistic and technical players who collectively create. The performing arts is one of the most collaborative fields in the world. All of this prolific creativity is born of both newly formed as well as tried and true partnerships between a myriad of players. The essential backdrop to fostering and strengthening those relationships is supported by meticulously directed social gatherings and celebrations, everything from "let's do lunch", to the Academy Awards Governors Ball.

My path has been a journey with a number of twists and turns, surprises and revelations. Throughout my career, my attitude has always been, "It's not what you get, but what you give", as well as, "Work hard". My life's journey thus far, combined with the blessing of boundless energy, defines who I am.

It's finally time to bring my experience home and share it with you. This book is your personal "All-Access Pass" to a comprehensive, behind-the-scenes look into Hollywood's event business, plus my unlikely trajectory to become part of it. Here is my take on the sneak-peeks, crazy stories, surprising facts, and stunning photography behind some of the most memorable celebrations in modern-day Hollywood.

Open the book to any chapter and go. I hope you enjoy.

Love,
Cheryl

Contents

CHAPTER 1

Italians in Mukluks

Dances with Bootsie

A FIVE-YEAR-OLD'S GUIDE TO INDIVIDUALITY, CREATIVITY, AND ADVENTURE

When I was very young, we lived in a modest duplex quite close to the "shatter cones", of Sudbury, in Northern Canada. Though shatter cones sound like Baskin-Robbins ice cream, that's what these bizarre rock formations were actually called. They provided clear evidence that Sudbury once had a violent dispute with an asteroid almost two billion years ago, and lost. Luckily, that was some time before my grandparents immigrated to Sudbury from Italy. At some point in my childhood, NASA geologists arrived to study this phenomenon with much interest, though at five years old, I knew none of this. I only remember how the rocky, alien landscape on the far side of the woods thrilled me.

Remember the '60s, when parents put their children outside with clear instructions to, "Go play"? The front door was unlocked, but we kids knew that we were free to romp around lunchtime. I wasn't a skipping-rope or a sand-box kind of girl. I had a craving for adventure; an intrepid spirit. I may as well have been going to the moon when I would disappear for hours on end, exploring and looking for signs of life. Sometimes, my beagle, Bootsie, would accompany me. Eventually I would find my way back to civilization, laden with pockets full of stones, holding an armful of sticks and quite happy with myself. My mother, exasperated as much as she was relieved, would demand, "Are you alright? Where have you been all this time? You are filthy!"

"Mum, I've been fighting the witches!" Like—how could you not know that, I would think. We've been over this...

I recall that the sticks were my weapons, and the stones, my bounty. My mother didn't get it. My young friends didn't get it. I'm not sure Bootsie got it, either. Mum would have none of it.

After several absences, Mum would yet again produce Bootsie's spare leash. I was consigned unceremoniously to the clothesline with a harness, alongside my canine companion. Our wings were clipped, though Boostie didn't much care. He was mostly retired. My forays into the unknown were now strictly restricted to the length of the clothesline, except on days my mother forgot to hook me up.

But not forever... I had lots of ideas.

PAGE 10
"Nono" Augustino
Cecchetto's 60th birthday
celebration

OPPOSITE PAGE
Family pictures to include
Dad with his six daughters

Famiglia, Love, and Laughter

FOOD FOR FUN

I am 100 percent Canadian-Italian. Though there's no Roman statuary on my front lawn, much of Italian cliché turns out to be largely true, and that's a good thing.

I sometimes wonder if my immigrating Italian grandparents, headed for the new world, had been told about the Canadian Indian summers, but not about the Canadian winters. A Cecchetto brother and sister, Augusto and Maria, each with their families in tow, immigrated by boat through Ellis Island more than 100 years ago. Both ventured north to Canada, seeking opportunity. Ultimately, Maria returned to settle in New Jersey. My grandfather, Augusto, remained in the land of the Great White North.

Don't get me wrong, I would never trade my Canadian roots. I love Canada and Canadians, and I've skied and snowmobiled just like any other red-blooded, frost-bitten Canadian kid. Every winter in my hometown, the snow often touched the eaves and we youngsters fancied ourselves as "Eskimos", burrowing snow tunnels from house to house. Every Canadian mother is adept at altering a Cinderella Halloween costume to fit over a snowsuit, earmuffs included. Out of necessity, Canadians invented the "tuque" and, by default, "hat hair". Modern version mukluks, boots with fake fur inside and out, were a fashion statement, sold to the masses at Simpsons-Sears.

Nevertheless, our young, largely empty and often frigid country must have come as quite the shock to those Italian immigrants who had lived all their lives in a country lapped by the Mediterranean, who spoke a language coined as romantic, and who had never stepped more than an olive branch away from a vineyard or a da Vinci. Considering the harsh Canadian winters, perhaps it was a more logical move for the Swedes and Finns who also immigrated to Sudbury in sizable numbers than the sun-worshipping Italians.

Sudbury hadn't yet dubbed itself "The Nickel Capital of the World" when my grandparents immigrated, and at that time it probably barely qualified as a city. At some point in my youth, the first freeway was built there, or rather, a bridge was, though it proudly boasted four lanes spanning the one train track that ran through town. The bridge was built in the '60s in anticipation of the four-lane highway that would connect the growing metropolis of Toronto—four hours to the south—with the mighty Northern Ontario industrial city of Sudbury. That's exactly what happened, albeit 40 years later.

Sudbury's largest employer by far was Inco, the mining company. Italian laborers flocked to Sudbury for jobs. Italian immigrants were very proud and committed to their adopted countries, and eagerly became citizens. After all, with no mass trans-Atlantic travel in the first half of the twentieth century, immigrants left their homelands expecting not to return. Nevertheless, North American Italians were never far from a pot of

OPPOSITE PAGE
From left: Sisters Carol, Cheryl, Corinne and Celia

Italians in Mukluks   15

pasta, an accordion, or a homemade bottle of wine. In that era, anyone courageous or desperate enough to leave their whole lives and cultures behind, with no advance promise of employment or prosperity, possessed a rock solid determination, and a sense of adventure.

My grandfather did not intend to work for anyone. By profession, he was a stonemason and in his new hometown started a construction business, Cecchetto Construction, without ever learning a word of English to the day he died. In my grandfather's day, approximately 18 years after the creation of the family business, the words "… and Son" were invariably added to the sign over the door, and a year or two after that, "… and Sons". My dad was predestined to be a builder.

Ours was a typical, big, Catholic family, all girls. Big families were natural to us. One might wonder what came first: the huge vat of simmering tomato sauce on the stove, or the many mouths at the table, eager to devour it. The fading, framed photos of my siblings and I depict baptisms, confirmations, communions and of course, large groups of happy, dark-haired people eating. We had the requisite *zios* and *zias* (uncles and aunts), *couginos* and *couginas* (cousins), and *nonis* and *nonos* (grandparents). Italians are a cohesive bunch; our blood is thicker than marinara. As our family grew, our guest count grew right along with us, like it or not (I liked it). In a large group, I always feel right at home.

We endured long winter months together, inevitably landing us indoors and at close quarters. When Italians get together, true to our reputation, we cook, have a lot of fun, fight, yell, talk too fast, and drink too much wine. Everyone is a welcome member of the family, related or not. Into my teens, I thought I was related to a number of people who were actually just good family friends. I called several older couples *zia* and *zio* who were not even Italian, but who in my heart were family to me. Those still with us are still *zia* and *zio*.

Dad built our house specifically designed to entertain, so that we could enjoy the many pleasures of family, and extended family life. He insisted on large rooms and open spaces. Construction was not a job for Dad; it was his art, his way of life. His ideas were ingenious, ergonomic, and beautiful. The casual dining room adjacent to the kitchen seated all of us comfortably and included a cut-out opening in the wall connecting to the kitchen counter on the other side. We set the table in the formal dining room on Sundays. The oversized living room was out-of-bounds and reserved for special occasions. We were the first family I knew with pullout kitchen cupboards that rolled out from under the counter tops for easy access. Dad built these innovative cupboards in the '60s. I always thought he had invented them, and maybe he did! He also wired up the downstairs TV so that he could turn it off from the kitchen with the flick of a switch when it was time for dinner. It was annoying, but Dad didn't call twice. Now that I'm a parent, I wish I knew his secret.

Sudbury summers are as warm and idyllic as Sudbury winters are cold and snowy. My father also built our "camp" on nearby Long Lake, which was essentially a rustic summer home with no winter insulation. When furniture, beds, dishes, or knick-knacks were replaced or retired from our home on Beaton Avenue, they were sent to the camp, only a 20-minute drive, but a world away.

Due to the Nordic influence in our region, Italians with cottages on the lakes surrounding Sudbury also built concrete steam baths down by their docks, copying the Nordic habit of taking a good steam, running along the dock, and jumping into the lake. Unlike the Swedes and Norwegians though, Italians tended not to

ABOVE
From left: Aduino (Dad),
Edwardo, Ogostino, Alfredo,
Maria, Almaldo, and
Zelino Cecchetto

indulge in the jumping into the lake part in the dead of winter, and Sudbury truly boasts the dead of winter. They did, however, learn to wear parkas, don snowshoes, ice fish, and hunt.

At some point, the Cecchetto brothers also built a more rustic "fish camp", as we called it: a cabin that was a brief floatplane ride to an otherwise inaccessible, uninhabited lake. In this pristine wilderness they fished and hunted deer, rabbit, pheasant, and duck—or at least the members of the family who didn't mind a bear scratching on the outside of the wall at night or a mouse running across a sleeping bag.

My parents loved to cook, which was apropos for a big Italian family and appreciated by assorted relatives, only a five-minute drive in various directions. I learned to cook at my parents' sides. Of course, next to that big pot of minestrone soup, one might also behold a freshly killed partridge or a plate of moose meat. Until they crossed the Atlantic, I don't believe many modern-day Italians were known for their hunting.

My Italian mum cooked, but her specialty was dessert, Nanaimo bars in particular. Mum always stashed several varieties of pie or desserts in our cool basement, already arranged on platters and covered with cellophane. In those days, people just showed up at your door for dessert and coffee, and an hour-long conversation about nothing in particular. I frequently showed up in the basement to steal a Nanaimo bar. They were heavenly. Mum was more prepared than any Girl Scout could ever hope to be, and her cold room would put any catering prep room I've seen to shame. There's no doubt I received my first degree in organization and event production from Mum.

The brothers also invested in a modest motel in Fort Lauderdale, where their families could go for respite from the bitter Canadian weather. The motel otherwise paid for itself. I remember we were once passing through the Toronto airport on our way to Florida, and were quizzed by the immigration officer about the contents of our large suitcases.

"Any wine?" the officer asked.

"Nope," said my father.

"Any meat?" the officer questioned.

"Nuh-uh," my father replied.

Once we landed and arrived at the motel, I'll never forget how Dad opened the huge suitcase, turned to me proudly, with a mischievous glint in his eye, and said, "Let's see… pepperoncino, capicola, prosciutto, cappellette, pepperoni, salami, and two, four, six… yeah, about eight bottles of homemade chianti!"

I loved it. We laughed hysterically. Then my father said gravely, "Cheryl, we are birds of a feather. You are the kind of person who will naturally get into a bit of trouble every day, so try to get into trouble by noon, and then you can take the rest of the day off."

Thanks for the heads up, Dad. His prediction turned out to be true. I'm not going to say what I stuff into my suitcases when I travel with my family to Canada. Let's just say that, yes, I do check in a number of bags. I can't imagine my father traveling today, paying $25 each way for each overly scrutinized and relentlessly X-rayed suitcase. I think he would've just headed back to the fish camp.

Dad was born in Sudbury on December 11, 1907. He passed in 1992, Mum in 1990. I still miss them. As I write this, Dad would have been 106 years old. His lessons live on.

I learned from my grandfather and my dad that it was perfectly natural to come up with an idea, turn it into a project, and literally build it from the ground up. Dad taught me to dream and bestowed upon me his imaginative and entrepreneurial spirit. Mum ran the whole world, right from our home.

The Writing on the Wall

Both my grandfathers commanded respect and attention, and were always the focal point of any family gathering. Whereas my paternal and entrepreneurial grandfather started the family construction business, my grandfather on my mother's side equally influenced me. He played the accordion.

Nono played the music of his birth skillfully and soulfully, and already at age three I was mesmerized. His classic "diatonic" accordion was equipped with only buttons, on the right and left faces, treble and base, and no keyboard. It was a difficult instrument to play and at the time I found it very exotic, as it lacked the familiar reference points of a piano. I couldn't understand how he was able to produce such beautiful harmonies with just those buttons that all looked the same. When Nono played, all other activity ceased, and everyone listened or sang along. The accordion is actually a formidable instrument. It is loud enough to be heard above a chorus of singers, or loud Italians, which in our case was usually the same thing. Perhaps more than any other instrument, an accordion's existence is to entertain, celebrate, and invite participation.

I always found my way to Nono. Family photos and home movies reveal me sitting as close to him as possible, even when he wasn't playing. I was attracted as much to his patriarchal energy, and the respect he always received, as I was to his music.

At age five, I begged my parents to buy me an accordion. They attempted to appease me with a plastic accordion from a toy store, believing my obsession was childhood whimsy. I'm told I played it relentlessly until it cracked. I begged them for another. Finally, at age six, my lessons began in earnest, with a full-fledged accordion. I studied with the virtuoso accordionist, Iona Reed, who was a world champion in 1967, and Ruth Johnson. Iona was married to Karl Pukara, also a brilliant accordionist. Karl was Finnish. I'm pretty sure that the Finns in Sudbury picked up accordion playing from the Italians. We stole the steam bath from them, so fair is fair. I have no idea why we were so lucky, but it was definitely a coup to Sudbury's accordion enthusiasts that such accomplished musicians happened to live in our midst. I've discovered that faithful students of Karl and Iona have posted many of their incredible, award-winning performances and competitions on YouTube. Take a look and listen to them; you'll be blown away. Watch the love of the music in their faces.

Iona reported to my mother that none of her students had ever played scales with as much fervor and force as I did. I honestly feel that I discovered and mastered basic discipline via such diligent practicing. I would often practice for four hours, my father faithfully at my side, apparently mastering one crossword puzzle after another, but actually supporting me with his company—just Dad and me. He would let out a little grunt or "oops" whenever I made a mistake. Over the years, my efforts paid off. I excelled and won a few awards of my own. At a very young age I was welcomed into a seasoned accordion orchestra. Together we played entire concertos, with various members playing assigned "instruments" via the switches on the accordion that change the sound, much like a church organ. We traveled around Canada and the U.S., performing and competing. I still look at the pictures and remember our retro gowns of colorful, patterned material, much like those matching outfits that the Von Trapp children wore.

My growing penchant to perform was not limited to when I was strapped to an instrument almost as big as I was. On long bus journeys with the orchestra, I would stand on my seat and entertain the troops with my best Louis Armstrong impression, then soak up all the cheering. I suppose I should have known by then where I was headed.

On more than a few occasions, my parents dragged me out of a deep sleep to perform the *Beer Barrel Polka* for guests, in my pajamas and slippers. Looking back, Mum and Dad, I'm so grateful I could play for you.

LEFT
Playing accordion with teacher, Iona Reed

The Roar of the Crowd

WHERE IT ALL BEGAN

So when did I develop this obsession to entertain?

Italian wedding showers are a big deal. In my family, we're talking 400 people. Our occasions were always played out at my Uncle Cassio's hotel, in the Venetian Hall. The hall featured a huge, stuffed sailfish over the head table. We thought it was big and fabulous, though now we realize that a stuffed and mounted sailfish in a landlocked mining town, 1,000 miles from the nearest ocean, is possibly a little weird.

Our occasions weren't the most fancy, but they were fun and loud. All the women added homemade items to the menu. We ate the requisite pasta and salad, told stories, toasted, ate again, and laughed so hard.

The appropriate wedding gift was always an envelope containing money for the bride and groom, preferably cash. Afterwards, the aunts (not the bride and groom) would go out together and buy 100 percent practical gifts with the money, such as Tupperware, an iron, a crockpot or frying pan. The mothers would always produce a photo book for the couple, dating back to when they were babies. In two and a half hours it was over. But what a two and a half hours!

I always assigned myself to spearhead the entertainment. Ahead of the party, I shanghaied everyone in my family I could as my accomplices. We entertained the crowd with a play that lasted anywhere from 40 minutes to an hour. I cast the company as various members of the celebrants' family, organized rehearsals, then obliged my actors to put appropriate costuming together. I wrote the script in which inside jokes that weren't necessarily very inside were revealed. I always played the mother, who relentlessly nagged and embarrassed her daughter, just as mothers are supposed to do. I hoped most of the performance could be heard above the ruckus.

At my sister Corinne's wedding, I, of course, played my own mother. Loudly. It was basically typecasting. Mum had mastered volume, which I fully emulated during my performance. Everyone thought I was hilarious, because they knew my mother so well. I knew her best, and I was pitch-perfect. Mum wouldn't talk to me for two days because I was spot on. She was so angry with me.

Our gatherings at the Venetian were a veritable cacophony of creativity, including not only my plays, but speeches, decorations, food, and of course, home-grown music. Nearly everyone in our clan played an instrument of some sort. I always fitted my accordion in somewhere. I witnessed how the all-encompassing nature of the celebration focused the family so that they would forget other obligations or distractions for a time and fully enjoy the environment, and especially reaffirming familial bonds. The promise of a terrific party often brought missing members of our extended family out of the woodwork, adding a reunion flavor to our gatherings.

A career in acting had never crossed my mind before the Venetian Hall. I was 16.

OPPOSITE PAGE

Cecchetto family gathering

What is it about Italians and shouting? When did we decide we had to drown out all the other Italians in the room? Are we worried that someone else may get a word in?

Our vivacious conversations require sweeping hand and arm gestures to drive home our inspired points of view, as if the shouting over each other wasn't enough. It is said that if you think you are speaking Italian, but aren't using your hands, you are just speaking French. I'm positive that any Italian would be a natural at the art of semaphore (communicating with flags). If anyone ever figures out how to perform semaphore loudly, it will be an Italian.

I've lost count of the times I've heard, "Cheryl you have such an outgoing personality", or "Cheryl, where do you get your energy?" or "Cheryl, can you slow down; I can't understand what you are saying."

My children actually ask me, "Mom, do you have to talk so loud? I'm right here."

I usually answer, "You have met my sisters, haven't you?"

Italians yell, usually at each other, from their passion, from the fire in their veins, and from very strong points of view. I learned to be loud just to keep up, just to be heard. My sisters will disagree that they are louder than I am. They can think that if they like. I love my family dearly, but I think I moved all the way to California in part just for the peace and quiet! Even so, during my first year of event production, my natural volume was apparently off-putting to a number of people, whom I discovered didn't want to work with me. California "chill" had not yet seeped into my hot pepper veins. I learned the hard way. On the west coast, I'm still the loudest person in the room. The upside is: you can always find me, and you will always know what I think. But I promise I will listen to you, too. Cross my hot, Italian heart.

OPPOSITE PAGE
Karl Pukara
Accordion Orchestra
Cheryl (2nd from left)

Rebel with a Cause

I DID IT MY WAY

At age 16, reigning in my free spirit and sense of adventure never crossed my mind, though by that time, I had long lost interest in the shatter cones, as well as outgrown both the literal and metaphorical limitations of the clothesline. Looking back, I suppose I was cultivating a penchant for thinking outside the box, taking risks, and sometimes not paying particular attention to standing rules.

It was a typical Friday night. I closed the front door loudly as I entered the house, several minutes before my 10 p.m. curfew. I phoned my best friends, Cheech and Shelly, and whispered into the phone, "I'll be over in 30 minutes." Then, much louder, "I'm hoooome!" So far, so good. At that age, as far as I was concerned, staying out all night wasn't risking my life, though in retrospect, perhaps it was. Either way, I was certainly risking my parents' wrath.

"Oh, I'm so tired," I said. "I think we played ping-pong for three hours! Good night." I yawned and kissed my parents, already in their bed and half asleep. I brushed my teeth and flushed the toilet. I closed the bathroom door, slightly louder than one should at 10 p.m. but not loud enough to be obnoxious, then went into my bedroom, leaving that door open. Years later, someone named Ferris Bueller took his day off; like him I quickly arranged my pillows and blankets to imitate me sleeping soundly in the shadows. Then I walked stealthily down the hall and into the kitchen. There was nary a creaking floorboard in the sturdy house my dad had built by hand (thanks, Dad!). Perhaps he should have left just one of them loose. Years before electronic security systems, and before the milkman went out of fashion, I carefully unlatched the milk box, then I slipped out of the front door, and locked it. I later returned through the milk box at six in the morning, having enjoyed five or six hours at someone's house party in between. I awoke at 8 a.m. because I had to waitress. I usually napped late on Saturday afternoon, because Saturday afternoon promised Saturday night.

I finally came clean about the milk box to my parents when I was 30, long after it had been covered in cement and Formica. Mum was miffed, but Dad thought it showed ingenuity.

OPPOSITE PAGE
Cheryl, age 18

Mum's Nanaimo Bars

INGREDIENTS

Base layer

½ cup (4 oz/115 g) unsalted butter

¼ cup (2 oz/60 g) sugar

5 tablespoons unsweetened cocoa powder

1 egg, beaten

2 cups (9 oz/260 g) graham wafer (digestive biscuit) crumbs

½ cup (2 oz/60 g) finely chopped almonds

1 cup unsweetened, shredded, dry coconut

Custard filling

¼ cup (2 oz/60 g) unsalted butter

3 tablespoons milk

2 tablespoons custard powder

2 cups (1 lb/450 g) confectioners sugar (powdered)

Chocolate topping

4 oz (115 g) semi-sweet (plain) chocolate

½ oz (15 g) unsalted butter

METHOD

To make the base layer

1. Melt the butter, sugar and cocoa in a heatproof bowl set over a pan of gently simmering water.

2. Add the egg and stir to cook and thicken. Remove from the heat. Stir in the crumbs, chopped almonds and coconut. Press firmly into an ungreased 8 in. (20 cm) square cake pan (tin).

To make the custard filling

1. Cream the butter, milk, custard powder and icing sugar together in a large bowl until light and fluffy. Spread over the base layer.

To make the topping

1. Melt the chocolate and butter together in a heatproof bowl set over gently simmering water. Set aside to cool, then pour over the filling layer and refrigerate to set.

2. Chill until chocolate has set.

3. Cut into squares and serve.

CHAPTER 2

The Great White North to The Great White Way

Wanderlust

THE BIG T.O.

I survived my teenage shenanigans, and in the late '70s I made it to York University, Toronto (known to Canadians as T.O), to study performing arts. My theatrical triumphs at family weddings and anniversary parties convinced me that I was destined to take the theatrical world by storm, and if there was an accordion world, then that world too.

One night, well into my final year at York, I was shooting tequila shots with my girlfriends when a burning question suddenly occurred to me; the question that hopefully hits most teenagers or 20-somethings eventually. I shouted over the music, "Do any of you know what you are doing with your lives?"

They looked up at me from their messy operation of cutting limes and pouring salt, with blank stares. To be fair, the thrust of the conversation had so far not evolved past counting each other's shots.

I repeated, "No, really. Seriously. What are we doing in life? What's your plan?"

The girls looked at each other and laughed, "Oh please Cecchetto. Have another tequila!"

I didn't. The prospect of another shot was suddenly unappealing. Sitting in our dorm's common area, I turned to my left and saw a brochure for George Brown College theatre arts program. In that tipsy, fleeting moment, my priorities shifted from girls-just-wanna-have-fun to a palpable resolve: the proverbial 'Aha' moment… I was actually having one.

I pushed the half-full shot glass of tequila in front of me to the messy center of the table and said simply, "I'm done with this." Holding up the brochure I said, "I'm going here." I had decided to take myself seriously.

I applied, on the final day of auditions, to George Brown College Theatre Arts program. I recited a monologue of a 54-year-old drug addict mother, from *Long Day's Journey into Night* by Eugene O'Neill. I played her to the hilt, in my sister Corinne's overcoat, which I think she inherited from my mother. Joseph Shaw, the artistic director, somehow concluded that, though he wasn't sure how, I would add a certain something to his class of 1980.

I developed my work ethic and determination at George Brown. I remember rehearsing the heck out of my solo for our production of *Jacques Brel is Alive and Well* and *Living in Paris*. Paul Horan, our mensch of a musical director assured me, "Cheryl, it's perfect. Don't change anything." The song suited my sensibilities, theatricality, and my expressive, alto voice. I wasn't satisfied, though. Was I a perfectionist, or simply scared out of my mind at the thought of performing in front of an invited audience, one that included my parents? I practiced it on my own well into the night. The next night, opening night, I was completely hoarse. Paul kept the key where it was and I sang the melody down an entire octave—not so much like Nana Mouskouri, more like Jacques himself, or Marlene Dietrich, in a raspy baritone. I think I wore Corinne's hand-me-down coat for that performance too. Thanks, Mum.

I was a go-getter. During college, everyone in my class longed to see theatre (notice the Canadian spelling). I contacted various theaters and found myself transferred right up to the decision makers, and scored tickets for my class on a number of occasions. "Hi, my name is Cheryl Cecchetto," I would say. "We are students at George Brown. We are Canada's next generation of actors, and we need to experience live theater so… basically… we would like some free tickets." More often than not, the answer was, "Yes, come pick up 20." It was actually easy. I probably should have noticed that even back then I was producing, making deals, putting things together. In retrospect, producer mode was when I felt the strongest, and most like myself.

At George Brown, I also discovered an interest in production, design and lighting. I was fascinated by how we could create a make-believe world; for example turning an empty space into an up-scale, turn of the century sitting room for a classic Michael Chekov play, with only basic set pieces: foam core, faux finish painting, and directed lights. I had no idea at the time how important to me this supposedly peripheral knowledge would be.

During the summer break from George Brown I auditioned for *The Water Safety Show*, teaching young campers the merits of not drowning. At one point we strapped on life-sized flat canoes over our shoulders, and shuffled a little soft shoe, with wooden paddles as dance partners. We had butchered the lyrics from the musical *Godspell*:

When you're all set (steppity step; steppity step)
To launch your canooooe (steppity step; steppity step)
Your P.F.D. (spoken) *Personal Floatation Device!*
Is fastened on youuuuu (kick, ball, change; kick, ball, change)

Hey, it was a paid gig before I even graduated, with all the grilled cheese I could eat and all the campfire songs I could sing. I was the envy of the George Brown class of 1980; I was a working actress. Enraptured, my Goddaughter, Sasha, four years old at the time, watched the entire show, and asked my sister in wide-eyed wonder, "Mummy, are there two Aunty Cheryls?"

In Toronto, post George Brown, I dove head first into auditioning. The first summer, I was cast in *One Big Break*, a dinner theater musical about actors trying to make it big—something that definitely resonated with me. The actors served the dinner, which I unfortunately also resonated with. Our mentor and restaurateur was Canadian performer Sandra O'Neill, whose claim to fame was, "The Longest Legs in Show Business". It was a world away from studying Stanislavsky. My buddy Bert, from George Brown, joined the show and I spent the rest of the run dodging him on stage, due to excessive arm choreography, as well as Bert's complete lack of awareness of his having the longest arms in show business.

The following summer I was cast at the Muskoka Festival, in Ontario's cottage country, two hours north of Toronto and two hours south of Sudbury. Everyone in my family came to see me wear a micro-mini, canary yellow dress, playing the loud and determined Lucy, harassing Schroeder at the piano in *You're a Good Man, Charlie Brown*. I had dragged Bert to that audition as well. In our case, the term "young company" actually

meant, "We aren't in a union, so we lug around our own sets", whereas the "old company" did not.

I was cast in the musical spoof *Flicks*, my first Actor's Equity (union) production. We enjoyed Equity wages, hot and cold running water, and somebody else being in charge of the set this time. At one point in the show I was to parody Marlene Dietrich, whom I was too young to have ever heard of. Someone in the cast did an impression of Marlene for me, so I played Marlene as an impression of my cast mate's impression.

Falling in love again… Never wanted to… What am I to do… I can't help it.

The audience laughed so I figured I did my job. I suppose I should finally check out Marlene on YouTube, singing her famous torch song, since I've played her twice. Sort of.

Bert and I also produced and co-starred in *The Owl and The Pussycat*, at The Pauline McGibbon Cultural Center, a fancy new name for Toronto's historic, converted morgue. Very courageous, I've always thought, to produce a play at the morgue, considering theater idiom:

That audience is dead.
We killed tonight.
I died out there.
We were slaughtered in the reviews.

We didn't die, creatively or otherwise, though Bert and I made a pact to never go down to the actual dressing rooms in the basement. Bert played Felix, a book-smart peeping Tom, and I played Doris, a street-smart, wannabe actress come call girl. My family came down from Sudbury to see that one, too. Bert and I still argue over who was the owl and who was the pussycat. I was the owl. It's my book.

One evening while attending an ongoing acting class in Toronto, my acting teacher and dear friend, Bob Barash, offered me some sage counsel: "Cheryl, it's time for you to go to New York." Yikes!

OPPOSITE PAGE
You're a Good Man, Charlie Brown.
Cast from left:
Tama Kossman,
Bert Hilkes, Scott Hurst,
Cheryl Cecchetto,
Greg Ernst and
Marianne Woods

If I Can Make it There

The brilliant and big-hearted Bob Barash, my acting teacher after college, felt that New York was where every aspiring actor must venture eventually, to make it big. Bob was an American, therefore partial to New York, where he grew up as an actor, spending much of his time at the fabled Actors Studio as one of the protégés of Lee Strasberg. Strasberg was the creator of the famous "method" style of acting, the bible for all aspiring actors at the time, and still highly influential.

Standing in the way of any Canadian actor pursuing a career in the U.S. was the coveted, infamous H1 work permit. The requisite hoop-jumping to obtain an H1 included comprehensive evidence of an artist's outstanding talent, as well as numerous credits of distinction. I undertook the project of procuring myself a permit with tunnel-visioned determination.

By the time I'm done, they will think I'm the greatest actress who ever breathed, I told myself. I sought out the 15 required letters of recommendation from each Canadian teacher and director I had worked with. Some had not heard from me for two or three years. I gently coaxed them into writing letters that were specific to the task at hand. They all responded faithfully with recommendations. I was very grateful. In some cases I fashioned a letterhead for those who didn't have their own, hopefully adding authority in favor of my case. I must admit, some of my credits of distinction were less than conspicuously distinct, nevertheless I felt that I had lived up to the letters attesting to my passion and work ethic—two attributes I inherited from Dad, who would say "Cheryl, how you do some things is how you do all things."

As I navigated the H1 rigmarole, the New York stage felt so much further away than just the 500 miles it read on the map. But somehow, it made me all the more determined. I hired the immigration lawyer recommended by my agent, completed all the paperwork, crossed all the 't's, dotted all the 'i's, and jumped through all the legal hoops. Finally, I received a formal letter from American Immigration that read something like this: *Completion of your application for an H1 work permit will require a notarized letter of welcome from the President of an American actors' union….*

"Oh, brother," my lawyer said. "American Immigration sure is making it up as they go." Convinced I was teetering on the edge of my career cliff, I looked to my one go-to person, who knew how to calm me down with his wise, patient, common sense advice, focusing me on the task at hand: I called my dad.

"You know, Cheryl," he said, his half-smile of certainty embracing me through the phone. "A closed door isn't a brick wall, even if it wants you to think it is. Your job is to open the door and walk through. Then there will be another door. You open that one next, and walk through, and so on and so on; just keep opening doors and walking through them. Doors are built with knobs and hinges for a reason. There's no such thing as a door that won't open, only one that is left shut." I decided to pay a visit to the President of the American Actors' Equity Association—the American theater union—in New York, in person, without an appointment. About a week later, in Manhattan, I sat very politely in the Actors' Equity President's outer office on West 46th Street, across from the secretary's desk. I was the only person there besides her. Eventually she looked up from her typing and considered me. She looked down again, presumably at the appointment book on her desk. Of course, my name was not on it.

"And you are…?" she asked; she seemed very sweet, but efficient, and very no-nonsense.

"Hi, I'm Canadian," I said. That apparently was not enough information.

"My name is Canadian… my name is Cheryl, and I'm Canadian. I've finished all of my paperwork to receive an H1."

She smiled… and waited.

I wasn't sure at that point whether or not I was going to run out of the room. In that moment, I remembered Mum's words to me before I had left on the 10-hour drive. "Cheryl, if this is what you want to do then I give you all my hope, and you'll still have all your hope, so you'll have double the determination and double the energy." I've wondered, many years later, if her hope for me was due in part to her never having had the opportunity to chase a dream herself, as she was very much a product of her generation. I cleared my throat.

"Everything has passed inspection and I've been offered provisional acceptance!" I gushed and I smiled my best smile back. I was shaking.

"Well, that's wonderful," she said. And then she waited.

It was my turn, again. "Um, so, Immigration now says I need an invitation into the country from the President of Actors' Equity."

Her eyes widened.

"So… is the President in?" I asked.

"You're Canadian?"

"Yes," I answered. This time she only waited a second. She inserted a fresh page into her typewriter and began typing. She paused from typing for a moment and looked up at me again.

"I'm Canadian," she said simply. She resumed typing.

"You are?" In that moment I felt 20 pounds lighter, even light-headed.

"Just a minute." She got up, snatched the letter from her typewriter, knocked lightly on the double door, and walked in. She returned in less than 20 seconds and handed me the letter.

"We Canadians stick together. Good luck."

And that was that.

The rumors are true. We Canadians really are some of the nicest people on the planet. Canadians talk over the fence and we bring each other pie. At least that's the Canada I remember, and it's the Canada I venture back to with my family. My sisters are the same. We get together, we cook, we laugh. Canadians do stick together. And have you noticed? We're everywhere.

Dad, I'm still opening doors and walking through.

Swimming Pools and Movie Stars

SHELLEY WINTERS

I was told to pick just one Shelley Winters story but I couldn't, I just couldn't.

In 1984, I packed my little AMC Pacer to the roof and drove to New York. I found an apartment full of male roommates who had no idea where the dish soap was or whether or not they owned a vacuum, and I got to work. I found myself a jazzercise class and a waitress job, and I hit the pavement, auditioning everywhere I could.

For the benefit of the under-40 crowd (or under 50?), Shelley Winters was a two-time Academy Award® winner from the Golden Age. In 1950, I believe, she was declared Hollywood's biggest box office draw of the year. Generation X may remember Shelley as the grandmother on the television program *Roseanne*. I remember how Shelley would marvel at how members of the younger generation would notice her on the street.

"Hey, there goes Roseanne's grandmother!" they'd remark to each other, surprised to see her in real life. Shelley would exclaim, "All of a sudden the kids know who I am. It's my second career..." Generation X and even Y did not know of her awards, or of her many decades of movie starring credits. These days the youngsters don't know Charlie Chaplin or Carol Burnett or Liza Minnelli. How old am I? I couldn't play a computer game to save my life, so let's call it even.

That same year, I applied for and was offered a coveted "observer" position at the legendary Actors Studio in New York. In exchange for performing various odd jobs at the Studio, observers were permitted to watch the acting sessions, which were otherwise "Actors Studio members only". Studio members would present scenes from plays in order to improve their skills. I had studied with a few of Lee Strasberg's protégés in Toronto. I remember how walking up the steps of the actual Actors Studio on 44th Street for the first time was akin to walking literally on hallowed ground. Marlon Brando, Marilyn Monroe, and Paul Newman had also climbed these steps to present scenes in front of Lee, or watch and learn from the master. Though Lee himself had passed on a few years before I arrived, I witnessed some amazing, intimate exchanges during my tenure there; the kinds of things that make a young actress pinch herself and ask, "Am I really here?"

As with everything, I was a very committed volunteer at the Studio, jumping in with whatever tertiary or technical job that had to be done, including signing in members arriving for sessions. I've always been an organizer, and I dive head first into whatever I am involved in. I've never had any problem putting in my two cents, problem solving, or thinking I could run things. I remember even hammering and painting at the Studio on occasion, which was never my forte. All observers harbored a completely transparent ulterior motive, which was to eventually audition and be invited as a lifetime Studio member.

One Monday, I was mesmerized as Ellen Burstyn (Oscar® winner for *Alice Doesn't Live Here Anymore*) executed a preparation exercise. Ellen first chose to practice a number of calisthenics moves, because they

OPPOSITE PAGE

From left: Cheryl Cecchetto,

Shelley Winters,

Lanie Kazan,

Menahem Golan and

Susan Strasberg

made her feel young and her character at that stage in the play was young. Then Ellen recreated, via her senses and imagination, her mentor. Ellen finished this exercise by sitting in front of the actual leather chair that Lee had sat in during sessions, weeping deeply at the loss of her mentor and father figure. This all led up to the fragile, emotionally fraught delivery of her first line in the play she was rehearsing, "I've made up my mind, Papa."

Ellen's entire preparation was intended to inform only her first line in the play. It was spellbinding to see the work of a true disciple and master of "The Method". I am sure at some point soon afterward someone must have finally got wise and donated Lee's chair to a museum, even the Smithsonian. If it wasn't Lee's actual chair, then it's a testament to Ellen's work that she made me believe it was.

One day I was working reception at the Studio, checking in members for sessions, when in walked Al Pacino. He greeted Ellen amiably and they chatted in front of me, just as everyday people do. I tried my best to be efficient, helpful and invisible, which has never been easy for me. Ellen usually moderated the sessions, which were Mondays and Wednesdays at 11 a.m. Moderating really means teaching, but at The Actors Studio everyone considers each other to be colleagues. Off the cuff, Ellen asked Al, "Do you want to do it?"

And Al replied, "No, you do it."

"Really? You can do it," Ellen insisted. They were casually debating who would moderate the most prestigious and sought-after classes in New York.

One Wednesday, the legendary and relentlessly impersonated Christopher Walken moderated. While he watched the scenes, he slouched as far back in his chair as one can slouch without falling out of it. And yes, in the notes after the work he did call the actress, "Dahling." In his notes to the actors, Christopher executed the best impression of himself I had ever heard. It was flawless.

I don't mean to name-drop. First names are how everybody addressed each other. Inside the doors of the Studio, the atmosphere was at once casual, with star-status left largely outside. The reverence for the work, however, was absolute.

Robert De Niro showed up in the back of the Studio during one session, which is where we lowly observers sat. At the end of this particular session, Shelley's ex-husband, director Vittorio Gassman, was to donate a very large television monitor to the Studio, and Shelley had asked Bobby to attend. I don't believe I ever heard anyone other than Shelley refer to Robert De Niro as Bobby. Bobby remained standing in the shadows behind the raised seating, incognito, assuming the posture of "I don't want anybody to talk to me". He never made his presence known, and slipped out before most had even realized he was there.

Another day, I sat in the balcony, watching Sean Penn chew his fingernails in the gallery below, as he watched intently.

At The Actors Studio, I felt like a fly on a very rarefied wall. We witnessed some remarkable acting in session, so long as we never spoke, nor occupied any of the good seats. For a young actress in New York, all of it was diary worthy.

Not long into my tenure as observer, I was in the restroom (we were allowed to occupy those seats) when I met, or rather, heard, Oscar-winning actress Shelley Winters for the first time. At this point I knew Shelley

Winters from the movies *Lolita*, *A Place in The Sun*, *The Diary of Anne Frank*, *A Patch of Blue*, and for those of you from my generation, *The Poseidon Adventure*. I also knew that Shelley Winters was one of the Studio's most famous members, whom I was bound to run into at some point.

From my single stall, I heard someone rush into the restroom, and breathlessly say, "I'm doing a scene. I gotta go. I gotta go!" It was definitely her. Shelley's voice was unmistakable. I froze. Maybe, I thought, I should vacate my cubicle in deference to what was apparently a Hollywood royalty emergency? The urgency in her voice seemed strong enough to justify my peeking around the door. There, for the first time, I laid eyes on Shelley Winters, perched contentedly over the sink. There was no possible response to that. This is not how I had envisioned my first meeting with a bona fide Golden Age movie star. I had no idea what to do, but I gingerly stepped out from behind the door. Offering "Hi, I'm Cheryl," seemed lame, at best. I assumed she would perhaps not be interested in meeting anyone new at that particular moment, though I was very decidedly standing right there, with nowhere to go, and with Shelley blocking my exit. It was Shelley who broke the ice. She looked up at me, didn't even blink, and said, "Hi, I'm Shelley Winters. When you gotta go, you gotta go."

It turned out that in June, Shelley was in need of a new assistant, though I hadn't heard of nor ever considered such a job. Apparently, David Hyslop, the Studio's stage manager at the time, with whom I had a feisty and fun relationship, had told Shelley, "There's only one person who can handle you, and you are the only person who can handle her."

Shelley cornered me soon after (not in the restroom this time), and said, "I want you to be my assistant. What's your name again?"

I blurted out, "Let me think about it." I didn't think for long. I was in New York to be an actress and who knew what opportunities, shortcuts, or at least unique experiences might follow, working for a Hollywood icon? I told Shelley, "yes."

Shelley called her assistants "Hit Girls". They each lasted about a year before they burned out. Shelley, many decades their senior, nevertheless ran them ragged. For me, as for most of them, it was a wonderful ride. Shelley and I were a good match from the start, though she was exhausting to work with. I worked for her for a whirlwind 12 months; we became friends for life. I wasn't so much her assistant, more her partner-in-crime, sounding board, script reader, driver, and sometimes chef. I directed the housekeeping, which, as a neat freak, I had found a little lacking. In a way, we were perfect partners, because we were both obsessed with whatever we were doing at the time; very focused, driven to succeed, and make our mark. Shelley was a phenomenal actress and consummate professional. Nothing stood in her way, not even an occupied restroom. I was determined to follow in her formidable footsteps and quickly learned that Shelley was not only enormously talented, but intelligent, hilarious, uniquely generous, outrageous, and with a heart of gold.

* * *

I discovered that Shelley kept two homes. One was on 72nd Street and Central Park East, overlooking Central Park, next to the famous Dakota building in which John Lennon had lived and was shot. The other was a house in the flats of Beverly Hills, on Oakhurst Street, right next to Santa Monica Boulevard. The names of these places were magical folklore to a recent transplant from small-town Canada. Initially, I worked for Shelley in New York, during the summer of 1986. Meanwhile, I also took classes and auditioned for whatever I could.

I remember sitting next to Shelley one morning when the actor Michael O'Keefe (with whom she had worked) tried several times to discreetly wave hello to her from across the theater as a scene was being presented. Shelley did not see him. I tried as best I could to connect them, whispering into Shelley's ear and pointing in Michael's direction until she shushed me quiet. Ever since, I've worried that Michael O'Keefe assumed he had been snubbed by Shelley Winters that day, when really he was just the victim of one of Shelley's nine pairs of glasses being forgotten on her night table.

"I want to see Leonard Bernstein in Central Park," Shelley announced in early July. Bernstein was to be conducting the New York Philharmonic. When the afternoon of July 4th arrived, the day of the performance, I called the garage to bring around the car. "No," Shelley said, "I don't want the car. We're going to walk."

"Shelley, are you sure?" I asked, "That is quite a distance." Occasionally Shelley went on a health kick, though usually short lived. "My doctor says I should walk. We're walking," she replied. I relented, because it was actually a welcome departure from her regular narrative of "I like everything that is bad for me."

With a group of her friends we walked slowly up Central Park West, stopping occasionally so that Shelley could rest for a bit on a folding stool that I had brought along. New Yorkers would stroll past, some lighting up in recognition, and she would say, "Are you going to watch the concert? I'll be right there." Shelley loved people.

The concert was wonderful. I remember one of the pieces was, of course, *The Star Spangled Banner*. Bernstein literally leapt into the air as he conducted. He was quite the showman and he knew it. His shoes smacked back down on the podium just as an orchestral phrase would hit us. We wept. Our little group sat on blankets in the midst of the crowd and snacked on our picnic lunch. Shelley sang, waved and cheered. Occasionally, someone on a nearby blanket would stand, snap a picture of her and then sit down again. People would look over and smile but nobody bothered her. That's New York.

One Monday, unbeknownst to Shelley, I conscripted her lifelong friend and Golden Age matinée idol Farley Granger. Farley and I conspired that she would hang out with him at his apartment for an afternoon, which was in the same building as hers, while I had Shelley's apartment completely steam-cleaned and scoured by four professionals with loud industrial equipment. I sprung "cleaning day" on Shelley the morning it was scheduled or she would never have allowed it. Shelley had a little difficulty with anything that wasn't her idea.

"Shelley, you are going down to Farley's," I said.

"Why? What are you talking about?" she demanded.

"Because the cleaners are here," I announced.

"Why are there cleaners here? What did you do?"

I said, "Shelley, if you ever wore your glasses, you would know…"

In October, Shelley announced quite nonchalantly over a turkey sandwich, "We are going to L.A. …"

"What?" I said.

"... to do the *Carson Show*," she continued.

"Oh, okay," I responded.

"… and stay the winter," she finished.

I hadn't considered leaving New York for the West Coast quite so early. I was stage trained. My teachers had drilled into me the value of stage work. They maintained that theatrical training and theatrical credits were the first order of business for a young actor, and they were right. I had planned for my first U.S. credits to be on (or off) Broadway. As usual, I had big plans as an actress, and I actually considered not going with her.

But, after much arguing and bribing, she assured me *ad nauseam*, "I'll help you with your career!"

I was off to Los Angeles with Shelley Winters.

ABOVE

Auditioning for the part of

Lucille Ball on Broadway

Shelley Winters' Marinara Sauce

INGREDIENTS

Chianti, for drinking

Extra virgin olive oil

1 shallot, chopped

2 garlic cloves, crushed

4–5 whole tomatoes, chopped

Sugar, to taste

Salt, to taste

Fresh basil leaves

Parmesan cheese

METHOD (SHELLEY STYLE)

1. Fetch several friends and glasses; open a bottle of chianti.
2. Pour a little extra virgin olive oil in a frying pan and set over a medium heat.
3. Sauté the shallots and garlic. Shelley always loved several cloves of garlic. Let them brown a little.
4. Keep talking, gossiping and laughing throughout.
5. Add the chopped tomatoes. Stir with love and don't stop. If the San Marino tomatoes were not in season, sometimes Shelley would buy the tomatoes that were available and add a pinch of sugar and then a dash of salt; though more often than not, just fresh tomatoes. She was generous with the basil, adding it at the very end. Shelley only served sauce over fresh linguini, which she bought fresh from the specialty grocery around the corner. Yes, you really taste the difference.
6. Serve with freshly grated (shredded) Parmesan and stories about old Hollywood.

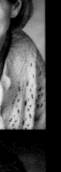

CHAPTER 3

La La Land

Palm Trees and Bit Parts

CALIFORNIA DREAMING

Shelley appeared on *The Tonight Show with Johnny Carson* about twice a year. Though she was obviously not hurting for cash, Shelley was a practical businesswoman, and thrifty. After all, her childhood had been decidedly Brooklyn lower class. Shelley timed her *Carson* appearances for her convenience because the show provided the airline tickets to fly back and forth, East Coast to West Coast, for the taping. She accepted an appearance whenever the time came for her to migrate between her apartment on 72nd Street and her house in Beverly Hills. *The Tonight Show* provided Shelley with a first class ticket. She would sometimes opt to cash in her ticket for a less expensive coach seat, thus covering the cost of an additional seat for her assistant. Though she sometimes played the diva, Shelley thought of herself as regular folk. Thus we flew with the regular folk, though Shelley's coach seat did not suit her high-maintenance back. At LAX airport, our flight attendants passed us as I walked, and Shelley limped, to baggage claim. They all smiled and said goodbye cheerfully, though she had not made their lives easy.

"Next time," they said politely, "sit up front!"

This first time I accompanied Shelley to *The Tonight Show,* I had long brown hair. Shelley was in hair and make-up when she suddenly decided then and there that she wanted me to cut my hair into a funky, Raquel Welch-esque hairdo that she thought would much better suit my face. Shelley was always thinking about my acting career, but I didn't take advice on my hair.

"You gotta be kidding me, what do you mean cut my hair? Shelley, you gotta go on set! Leave me alone. They want you backstage… you gotta be nuts!" I blurted.

"I am not going on. You need to cut your hair. It looks terrible and you look frumpy! You are no longer in Alaska! Let me talk to the hairdresser," she replied.

"I'm not from Alaska, Shelley. I'm from Sudbury, Canada," I said.

"Well, who's heard of Sudbury?" Shelley responded.

"Well that's where I'm from," I replied.

"Just cut off your hair, Cheryl! You look like a trapper from the Canadian bush," she stated. I don't think it was ever Shelley's intention to be rude. I often witnessed her perform acts of incredible kindness. But she was always relentlessly direct. Shelley pulled no punches.

At that moment, Johnny Carson walked in to say hello. Shelley received this type of courtesy from bigwigs in the industry all the time. She was a "regular" on the show.

"I can't go on yet. This is my assistant Cheryl Chechetti…"—Shelley could not pronounce my surname—"… and she won't cut her hair. Just look at her. It's so 1970s!"

The Tonight Show, as most talk shows still are, was "live to tape", so there was no waiting or postponing, not even for Shelley Winters. Johnny looked at me and smiled, "Well, how would you like to get your hair cut, on me?" How was it that the fate of *The Tonight Show* was falling onto my shoulders?

I buckled under the pressure, turned to the hairdresser and said, "Would you just cut off my hair so we can get on with the show?"

She did, and we got on with the show.

I liked the haircut, too.

That year, the day before Thanksgiving, Shelley decided to throw a Thanksgiving party. When the following afternoon arrived, 50 people showed up—pot luck style. A few stars came but mostly lots of regular folk, including many observers from the Studio, the young actor hopefuls. Shelley was the consummate den mother. She picked up a lot of "strays" and surrounded herself with colorful, creative, and often wacky people. Shelley had East and West Coast families, and everyone loved her.

Once, we were shopping in West Hollywood. Shelley liked shopping, but she usually ended up looking for clothing for me, as opposed to herself.

"Put this on!" she'd say, and I'd find myself walking in and out of a dressing room, trying on various outfits as Shelley sat in a chair the store had found for her and critiqued. Somehow, Shelley always managed to corral four clerks into serving her, all of them thoroughly enjoying themselves as she held court.

On one occasion, as we left the store, me carrying an outfit I wasn't sure that I liked, we both noticed a little homeless boy and his mother on the sidewalk, neither of them wearing any shoes. Shelley being Shelley, she could not let this stand. We walked two blocks to Payless Shoes and bought, I don't know how many, perhaps 20 pairs of shoes. Unwilling to disregard the obvious, I said, "Shelley they're homeless, where they heck are they going to put all those shoes? Just give them one pair of shoes."

She calmly replied, "Cheryl, they can give them to their friends who need shoes."

Soon I found myself next to her conspicuous Lincoln convertible, white on the outside and blood red on the inside, with the roof down (always), parked on Sunset Boulevard in the red zone with Shelley handing me box after box of shoes. We left the mother and son with two or three towers of shoes. As was so often the case with Shelley Winters, whenever she departed the scene, people didn't know what had hit them. Shelley always made the proverbial great exit.

Another day we were driving in West Hollywood and Shelley decided that she wanted to make a red sauce of chopped tomatoes and garlic: so simple and so delicious. Shelley does nothing small, so we bought a few crates of tomatoes. We also bought a tree, simply because she saw it in a pot in front of a store and she wanted it for a spot in her entrance. It was a really big tree in a really big tree pot, but Shelley, very much into immediate gratification, would not wait for delivery. So, I'm driving, Shelley's behind me with the tomatoes and holding the tree, and she starts complaining about her back.

"I can't hold the tree, it's blowing in the wind!" She had this long, drawn out voice. "I can't do this, my back's killing me; I gotta drive."

And I said, "Shelley, you don't drive."

ABOVE
Lee Marvin and Chuck
Norris filming *The Delta Force*
in Tel Aviv, 1986

"I'm driving! Don't tell me what I can't do. You work for me." She would always say this to me. We would laugh so hard, and fight so hard, but mostly laugh. "Why am I paying you?" she'd ask, "I entertain you non-stop. You should be paying me."

The wailing continued until I finally pulled over; we had only about 15 blocks to go.

And Shelley drove. I'm telling you, Shelley didn't stop at a single red light or stop sign. She didn't. She kept jerking the car left and right, gas and break, because she hadn't driven in so long. She put her left foot on the brake and her right foot on the gas at the same time. Meanwhile, I'm screaming at her, demanding that she stop the car. If I hadn't been so scared, I would have been sick. And forget the tree leaning in the wind. I couldn't have cared less about the tree. Forget the tomatoes. I was just trying to get out of the car, waving and screaming at everyone around us to get off the road, at least to save themselves. I kept begging Shelley to stop.

Somehow we made it home in one piece with the tree and the crates of tomatoes. I slammed the door on that convertible and stormed toward the house, with her screaming at me, "Where are you going? Help me with the tomatoes!" I didn't even look back at her.

"We. Are. Not talking. For the rest of the day," I said loudly, trembling. I was so furious. My short life had flashed in front of me.

Three or four hours later, after I cooled down, I came out of my room (I used to live in her home). I had honestly thought that I was going to die. What was I going to do with this woman? It was a miracle we had not been accosted by the police. I was a little Canadian in a big city with my little temporary work permit, living with a completely crazy movie star. Whose life was this, anyway? I just wanted to be an actress.

I went into the kitchen and saw that Shelley had carried the tomatoes in herself, bad back and all, and made three huge pots of tomato sauce. I don't remember how the potted tree eventually found its place in the

ABOVE
The Delta Force
From left: Martin Balsam,
Cheryl Cecchetto,
Joey Bishop and cast member

hallway. The room looked like there had been a tomato fight to the death. But Shelley sat there, glowing like a young child with a grin on her face from ear to ear and her wise, gentle eyes beaming. She could just melt your heart.

Shelley said to me, "I made you my tomato sauce. Should we have a party?" We prepared salad, pasta, and garlic bread. Those were Shelley's favorite things. Fifty people showed up, many of whom also brought homemade dishes. Shelley sat in the kitchen and talked to us.

Shelley was offered a part in *The Delta Force* with Chuck Norris. The movie was largely based on the 1985 rescue of the hijacked TWA flight 847 and the female flight attendant, Uli Derickson, who eventually convinced the hijackers to release all the hostages.

Shelley announced, "Where's your passport? We're going to Israel."

An opportunity to fly first-class to Israel with a gaggle of famous actors, stay in a five-star hotel with my own room and a *per diem*, all sounded quite extraordinary to my 20-something self. The actress in me, however, sensed that, if I played my cards right, there was another opportunity lurking here. I had been dabbling in EST (Erhard Seminars Training), a life-skills training movement at the time. There was a lot of self-help dabbling in California in the '80s, from meditation to yoga, and Jane Fonda jazzercizing to juice fasts. EST, later called The Forum, was very California. My EST buddies counseled me on how to negotiate my response to Shelley.

A few days later, I marched into Shelley's living room and announced, "I'd love to go to Israel, but only if I get a part in the movie."

As you can imagine, Shelley just blew off the handle. "Who the heck do you think you are? You are an assistant! You've got your nerve!"

I said, "I understand what you are saying, Shelley, but I really need my SAG (Screen Actors Guild) card and this will do it."

"You work for me!" she yelled.

"I know. But this is a win-win situation. You'll have your assistant in Israel, and I'll get my SAG card and a credit in a Menahem Golan film!" I replied. Menahem was a big producer and director in th 1980s.

"Absolutely not," she declared. "What am I supposed to do, march into Menahem Golan's office and tell him I'm not going to Israel unless he gives my assistant a part in his movie?"

The next day, Shelley tells me to get in the car. So, I got in the car, but we drove to Menahem Golan's office. She barged right in and proclaimed, "Menahem, this is Cheryl, my assistant. I'm not going to Israel unless Cheryl gets a part in the picture." (Shelley always called movies "pictures", a throwback to Hollywood's Golden Age.)

So I got a part in the "picture". There was really no big part for me, but I got a week's pay at SAG rates, my flights were provided, my expenses included, and I was being paid by Shelley as well. She thought I was the biggest operator of all time.

I did have a couple of scenes. At one point in the film, Lainie Kazan, Susan Strasberg and Shelley are all crying as their hostage husbands are taken off the plane to an unknown fate. Just before we shot this, Menahem Golan had announced to our little group, "Okay! Where are my Actors Studio people? I need some crying!" I must admit, the movie depicted cruelty to innocent people, so every time the camera rolled, I would find the situation upsetting. But I was also crying because I wanted to be in a movie so badly, and finally I was! If you watch the scene closely, I am watching and crying from the back of the plane… to nobody in particular.

At one point in Israel, Shelley was upset with me for a variety of reasons, but probably mostly because I won 100 bucks worth of shekels from her in a game of Gin Rummy. Shelley could be very competitive. We were arguing in the elevator on the way to our room after an infamous match with Lainie Kazan, Susan Strasberg, and Lee Marvin. Shelley couldn't believe I was winning so much and was really miffed that I was getting paid in three different scenarios: as an actress, an assistant, and now in card games. She was laughing and yelling all at once, when she got off on the wrong floor.

I held the elevator open because I knew that we weren't on the correct floor, but I couldn't get a word in to tell her. Meanwhile, she talked and complained all the way down the hall, walking up to the wrong door, shouting, "Come on and open up the door, Cheryl! I need to get into my room!"

And I replied, "Shelley… um… Shelley? This is not our floor, Shelley."

So naturally someone comes to the door of the room, a young couple, and she starts yelling at them, "What the heck are you doing in my room? Get out!" Meanwhile, I'm hiding back in the elevator. At that time, Shelley had quite a bit of notoriety, especially with the older crowd. Imagine discovering Sally Field banging on your hotel door today.

Bravely, I poked my head out of the elevator again and called out, "Shelley, it's not your room."

"Don't be telling me it's not my room," she replied.

And I'm yelling down the hallway right back at her because it's not her room. Suddenly we are laughing, and then we are laughing all the harder because of the confused and slightly scared looks on the faces of the guests whose room she had besieged. Between peals of laughter, Shelley squealed out to me, "Oh… I've peed in my pants just a little," and we can hardly stand up. She finally removed herself from the wrong doorway and made it to our rooms, but it was a movie in itself trying to get there. It took us 30 minutes to compose ourselves.

"Before you die," my father told me, "you are going to look back at your life and you are going to count on five fingers the people who really, really had an impact, who shaped it as much as you did, who touched and challenged you, turned you upside down, helped you discover who you are, who were unrelentingly loyal, and who you will never forget."

Shelley, you are my thumb, hands down. Love you forever.

Food of the Gods

AMBROSIA

As Shelley's *Hit Girl de jour,* I lasted 12 months, which was the average. I was itching to get on with my acting career and Shelley commanded all of my attention, though she wanted me to be a success as much as I did. Once working full-time for Shelley came to an end, I did faithfully pursue my acting career. I took classes with a number of teachers. I buzzed around town dropping off resumés to agents when I heard about appropriate parts. This was pre-internet, when resumés were hand delivered, and when it was much easier to get onto a studio lot. You could drive up to the gate and say you were a courier—which was actually true; a courier working for yourself. Delivering was incredibly time consuming. I paid a secret, monthly fee to pick up a list of the available parts every day from inside my contact's screen door. It felt very clandestine and exciting; even dangerous. I laugh now at how innocent it all was. How ridiculous was it to prevent actors from applying for jobs by hiding the available parts from actors? I submitted myself for everything I could. I was a better manager than the manager I hired to find auditions for me. That should have told me something right there.

I actually did experience an occasional taste of working as an actor inside the studio gates, and I have to admit it was thrilling. I was a client on *L.A. Law,* waiting for parking validation from my lawyer, Arnie's secretary, and then meowing at the very handsome Jimmy Smits. That was actually one of my two lines: "Meow."

I also played the accordion as a boisterous, off-the-boat Italian relative of a middle-aged rookie cop played by Paul Sorvino, in *The Oldest Rookie.* I think I walked into the audition room playing the accordion… that cinched the deal. I was particularly glad that day that I had lugged my accordion all the way from Canada, via New York.

I played a jailed hooker on *The Golden Girls*. That was great fun, because it was shot in front of a live audience, and I bowed with the rest of that iconic cast at the end of taping, along with guest star Burt Reynolds.

Yet, while I was auditioning I needed that proverbial survival job. I discovered that Hollywood, the heart of Los Angeles and the "Entertainment Capital of the World", was also the "schmooze capital of the world" and so, by default, also the "catering capital of the world". Producers, actors, and their handlers love having everything brought to them literally on silver platters. The infamous phrase "Don't quit your day job" is a misnomer, when applied to the acting profession. An actor must be available during the day for all that "pavement pounding" you've heard about. I chose to take a job in the catering industry because the shifts are mostly at night. After working briefly with a number of catering companies, I decided to go with a premiere company, Ambrosia.

The day after I worked at my first Ambrosia party, I told Carl Bendix and David Corwin, the company's co-owners, "I want to manage for you," and the die was cast. That first night, they had noticed my organizational skills (as well as my tendency to take over) and so they assigned me to manage many of their parties. Most

Ambrosia parties at that point were smaller affairs in private homes. As the company grew, so did my responsibilities.

Working for Ambrosia was less like a job and more like going to summer camp. Off-premise catering, essentially for those parties not in hotels or restaurants, was just coming into its own. Best friends, Carl (Ambrosia's heart and brilliantly creative spirit) and David (the left-brained, and technical ideas guy), set the tone. Their partnership eventually elevated them to one of the top catering firms and party designers in the city. The staff were the campers, Carl and David were the camp councelors and we called ourselves "Ambrosites".

As Carl and David's company grew, I was managing, and sometimes organizing, larger and larger parties, while also auditioning during the day. At the same time, the Academy of Motion Picture Arts and Sciences had been pining to relocate their fabled Academy Awards® to a much larger venue, in order to host their black tie Governors Ball under the same roof. No hotel in the city was big enough for the party.

Enter Carl Bendix. Carl was a visionary; a bit of a mystic and an Ashram attender. In L.A., an Ashram is basically a Hindu-inspired group of benevolent devotees who meditate together, eat mostly vegetarian food, seek peace and enlightenment… and dress comfortably. At the Ashram they called Carl "Galesh", a name I'm told is straight out of the Kabbalah, before anybody knew about the Kabbalah. Carl was the real deal and believed only in possibilities, providence, and the word yes. He pitched the Academy Awards Governors Ball first off-premise catering contract. The Academy said "yes".

Carl then turned to me and said, "We are serving lamb to 1,700 guests from a big kitchen tent in the parking lot of the Shrine Auditorium Expo Hall. Go." What he didn't mention was that the Shrine was a cavernous space completely devoid of anything resembling party equipment.

The Expo Hall is the size of seven basketball courts. Carl handed me a list of the names of 500 waiters and kitchen staff and said, "There you go. Organize this. I'll be over there, chanting…" (Okay, I jest about the chanting part and I can just hear Carl calling me when he reads this…).

I said, "Carl! Wait, organize what?" Remember me? I'm the girl from small-town Canada who followed a movie star to Beverly Hills to become an actress. "Where did you find 500 waiters and kitchen assistants? Who are these people?"

"Relax, Cheryl," Carl answered. "The stars will align. I'll be right back." Carl walked back into his office. I think a rainbow followed him. Alone and dumbfounded, I tried to comprehend what I was being asked to do. There was no template, as far as I knew. I had to invent one.

In an empty, unfinished office at Ambrosia, I drafted Kim and Corine, Ambrosia's equipment room managers.

"Please fill out these post notes, with one waiter's name on each. We'll stick every name on the wall," I said, "360 degrees around us." There was no such thing as Excel spreadsheets or computer-generated drawings at that time. They thought I was nuts. I possibly was.

"Cheryl, you're nuts," they affirmed.

"I know," I said.

Computers, in those days, were essentially typewriters with a little attitude and, if really high-tech, a small green screen. I think at this point Steve Jobs was still barefoot and working in his garage. What's worse, at the

time I was only aware of the existence of yellow Post-it® notes, so we found ourselves surrounded by a sea of glaring yellow. We laughed so hard.

Carl walked into my "office" a day later, blowing several Post-it notes from their positions, and I said, "Carl! You just killed 10 waiters." He laughed, and closed the door again.

"I've got it!" I yelled so loud that Kim and Corine dropped a few more waiters, and scrambled to relocate their rightful positions on the wall. I walked around the room and plucked all the names of the people I knew in catering who had heads on their shoulders. I was eventually holding twenty sticky notes in my hand. As I counted those precious papers I said, "We'll turn the party into twelve… thirteen… twenty small restaurants, each self-contained."

"Get real! Twenty parties instead of one?" Kim and Corine were ready to jump out of the first floor window, obscured as it was by Post-it notes.

"It will work," I insisted, with an unfettered determination disguised as conviction—not the same thing. The twenty were appointed area managers. Other names we recognized were assigned as section captains and others became servers. Those remaining were assistant waiters, there to offer beverages and bread. The names none of us recognized at all I would insulate from the guests as much as possible. They would be food runners.

I drew up dish lines within the dimensions of a big, rented kitchen tent. Dish lines are essentially long, rented tables, manned by chefs and kitchen assistants on both sides. Dinner plates are slid along the table, with each attendant offering another item to the plate. Essentially it's the catering version of Henry Ford's assembly line. I stand to be corrected, but if I didn't invent this system outright, 28 years ago, then I was oblivious and re-invented it all over, this time for a high-end dinner served from an ersatz kitchen in an oversized tent.

My kitchen and ballroom formulas and layouts began to take shape on two huge diagrams, which eventually replaced the Post-it notes. The Expo Hall requirements included tables, chairs, linens, flowers, glassware, carpeting, lighting… and all were added to an ever-lengthening rental order.

I felt a palpable excitement about my burgeoning creation. I found the process at once to be creative, and very scientific. It suited me. I had jumped in with a wing, a prayer and an A+ in math. To my delight my floor plans of the Expo Hall, its smaller kitchen and the huge kitchen tent in the parking lot slowly took shape, though it wasn't brain surgery. On the diagram, rented kitchen equipment of every description was placed with military precision, with the help of another mentor of mine, Jeff Williams, Vice President of Regal Rents, the largest party rental company in Los Angeles.

Meanwhile, Carl, right-brained and wonderfully creative as he was, did not see the world as strictly structured as I did. Carl announced that he would place crystals on each table, focusing the energy so that everything would flow in beautiful harmony. That was Carl's process. The muses would join us, the angels would sing. Carl was on a first name basis with a guru advisor, and as far as he was concerned, a number of angels besides. The room would be visually stunning.

On the day of the show, five hours before we opened the doors for the guests, I ventured outside to check on the food side of things. Carl had pulled up in a 40-foot Winnebago, displacing a noticeable chunk of the outside kitchen, the area reserved for grilling. He emerged, triumphantly from his victory chariot (wearing a Caftan? May as well...), brandishing a glass of bubbly.

"Carl, what in God's name are you doing?!" I asked.

"Cheryl, I brought you some champagne. Here, try this caviar, it's divine," was his reply.

"Carl, are you nuts? Nobody has time to eat caviar! What happened to the kitchen?!" I asked. He didn't hear me, with all the harps playing in his head.

"I need 20 waiters to carry the crystals into the ballroom, and I will arrange them," he said. Through the door of the Winnebago, I could see several silver buckets of champagne and between them even more plastic buckets of crystal rocks. I breathed deeply.

It's okay, I thought. I won't have a nervous breakdown, I won't, I won't. I don't have time… okay, one sip of champagne to calm my nerves. I needed it.

When guests arrived, we were ready, with everything and everyone organized in symmetrical perfection, facing the entrance of the ballroom. The room looked fantastic. Waiters stood in their places. Among them stood the captains, that year dressed in military jackets, epaulets, and maybe even military hats. Yes, really. It was the '80s.

Carl had hired a "celebrity" chef, famous for his grilled lamb, whom he flew down from San Francisco. Apparently the chef had only grilled lamb for up to a hundred people. Dinner was twenty minutes late. At this point, I pretty much had a well-deserved, well-dressed nervous breakdown, though I resisted another glass of champagne. I also resisted running into the kitchen to throw a bunch of pointy-edged crystals at the chef AND Carl. One must adapt and conquer, so I ran to the orchestra and demanded dance music.

"In The Mood!" I yelled to the conductor, even though I decidedly wasn't. I plucked two waiters from the fray and told them to dance. They did. Guests happily joined in.

It was a beautiful evening; the celebrities who mingled all around us thoroughly enjoyed themselves. The lamb was delicious, and worth the wait. The crystals had worked. The Oscars® solidified the Ambrosia family closer than ever. Carl and David—creative, courageous, generous and playful—divined the fun and camaraderie in all of us Ambrosites. That first Governors Ball created business relationships and friendships among us, lasting to this day, even as most of us have moved on to different walks of life.

Of course, I exaggerate a bit about my dear friend, Carl. Thirty years ago Carl Bendix and David Corwin started Ambrosia in a row house, by the beach in Playa Del Rey. Their neighbors would arrive home from work in the afternoon to discover their ovens were full of hors d'oeuvres, baking away for Carl and David's gig that night. Carl is still at the helm of Ambrosia Productions—a full-scale, event production company, serving studio heads and American Presidents. David, an award-winning projection designer and media producer, heads Megavision Arts. I learned more about creativity, courage, generosity and fun from those two than they will ever know.

What Happens in Vegas...

LOADED DICE

In the early '90s, Ambrosia's visionary Carl Bendix and mastermind David Corwin took on a ginormous convention luncheon in Las Vegas for McDonald's Corporation. Carl and David pitched their plan and McDonald's agreed that nobody could do it like Ambrosia could.

The whole Ambrosia gang jumped on board. Road trip! We were in for a nice chunk of income to support all of our acting and artistic aspirations. I don't know if you've ever been in one of those huge, hotel gambling lobbys with the old-style slot machines? Many of us looked forward to gambling a roll of quarters, or two, or three, amongst the din of all the flashing lights and ringing bells, just to see what all the fuss was about.

The guest count was 15,000, maybe more. No joke. I have a mind for figures, but I blocked out that one long ago to stop the night sweats. Only a football stadium could host the convention, and only the parking lot of a football stadium could accommodate the sprawling catering compound required to feed it. We were contracted to serve the masses a single picnic-style, barbecue lunch, after which they would return to the stadium for the remainder of the day.

Arriving at the sprawling parking lot on the first day of set-up, I swear I could see the curvature of the Earth. Ultimately, I worked on rollerblades for three days, 15 hours a day—the last day weaving through and around some very peeved guests (not because of me). I'm a multi-tasker. I loved orchestrating the whole thing and making the money, while simultaneously getting a good workout. Win, win and win. It would be great fun. Las Vegas didn't think so.

The immensity of the operation begged the hiring of two hundred local staff. Not well versed in the off-premise catering lexicon, let's just say that the Las Vegas casual workforce proved a challenge. Via a number of local staffing services, we searched high and low to fill our waiter needs. During the days prior, I purchased many a drive-thru order of McNuggets, tacos and deep fried chicken buckets. My ulterior motive was to call through the service window, "Hey! Who wants to work for me on Thursday?"

Hiring and training candidates in fifteen minutes to serve a buffet is less than ideal. I swallowed hard as I contemplated the Grand Canyon of space between the enthusiasm and the experience in some cases. This would prove difficult. The attitude and gratitude of Las Vegas' casual workforce was mostly terrific, but clearly one of the staffing agencies we contacted did not keep a roster of people well versed in the food service industry.

I insisted that buffet attendants expose less than 20 percent of any inked skin. Call me old-fashioned. Males with nail polished fingers would only run food, not serve it. Call me old-fashioned again. Flip-flops were not acceptable. I also signed two court-ordered, community service papers. I wasn't sure how serving lunch to a convention could be construed as community service, but I wasn't rocking the boat at this point.

A good amount of young people had or did work at one of the hotels in town and knew what they were doing. Some were not so young, and really knew what they were doing. Many of those I assigned to supervisor positions on the spot, as there was a lot of ground to cover. Even those few from the Goth crowd were mostly very sweet people, albeit sporting bold, creative fashion statements. I thought I was the one who enjoyed experimenting outside the box.

Ex-valet guys were especially adaptable and moved like the wind, until the heat caught up with them. In the two days of set-up, half of the advance staff had developed borderline heat prostration. Everyone had that in common; to quote playwright Neil Simon, it was "Africa hot". The endless asphalt beneath our feet likened more to a griddle, and we were the pancakes. The waves of heat rippled on the pavement. Hotels floated above the ground on the Strip in the distance. One of the staff rode around in a cushy golf cart in *Lawrence of Arabia* fashion. The cart was decked out with a little canopy, laden with water bottles and sporting an annoying horn, which he utilized generously. He handed bottles to anyone on the tarmac who would accept them. Most of them wanted his job, riding around in the breeze, under the shade.

"Drink before you're thirsty, or it's too late," he repeated.

"Oh, right, thanks, never thought of that."

"I haven't been to the porta-potty all day today, have you?" I asked Carl.

"Only in the morning," he replied from under his Indiana Jones hat.

Suddenly, a frantic call came over the radio, "Nancy Gulla has fainted!" Nancy, of the Ambrosia inner circle, was one of our best table designers. The emergency medical technicians (EMTs) were called. Nancy languished in the back of their vehicle. While the red lights flashed, Nancy sipped electrolytes gingerly from a straw as all of us huddled nervously around the vehicle. Would we all drop like flies, one by one?

A handsome EMT called back to his base on their radio, "…been working in the sun, complaining of dizziness and nausea, approximately 38 years old…" He didn't finish.

Nancy bolted up from her heat-stroked stupor to yell, "34!" thus reclaiming four precious years before she melted back into the gurney. Nancy would be okay. In Hollywood, one year is pretty much seven "actress years". Mental note: "Cure for heat prostration: Take two handsome EMTs and call me in the morning." We laughed so hard, which we always did at Ambrosia.

Las Vegas did not think it was funny.

The day before the event, we were called downtown by the health department. "Downtown" did not mean the Las Vegas "Strip". This was the decidedly grey downtown Las Vegas that nobody knows about. Their summons was bizarre to say the least; we had provided the required specifications months before, filled out various documents and paid a hefty fee. Plus, Ambrosia were experts at the off-premise event template in Los Angeles. Scratch that—Carl had effectively invented it, or at least refined it from its rudimentary, mass-cafeteria roots, raising it to A-List standards. Carl and David knew all there was to know about permitting, health standards and fire marshals. Itching to get back to work, we re-answered numerous questions, answered a few new ones, and received the stamp of approval a second time.

Our "refer" (refrigerator) trucks, locked up tight and running all night, had been spread strategically around the compound, holding the food at the legally required temperature. In the morning and on schedule, we opened the doors of the refers, whereupon salad ingredients, burgers, and hot dogs were carried and golf-carted to their various prep areas. Suddenly, a Dodge Dart with an official-looking decal, too large for the door, pulled up. Men wearing serious expressions, decked in white smocks, plastic gloves and armed with space-age thermometers stepped out. They descended ominously upon our hapless refers. I don't know if the plastic gloves were to protect the food, or the men inspecting it.

The shortest guy in a wannabe HazMat suit emerged from the closest refer and proclaimed, "The trucks are not cold enough; you cannot serve this food."

Carl had a meltdown, and I was right behind him. The Ambrosia buffet managers in my vicinity went into shock. It was 10 a.m. and lunch was at noon. Braving heat stroke for three days, I noticed how invested in this party I had become. I begged and bargained with the Health Department officers, who brandished their unyielding thermometers in their plastic pocket protectors. I have tremendous respect for the Health Department, but these men had arrived without any knowledge or precedent with regard to an off-premise event. They ignored our permits and their specifications, and my sense was that they were making up the rules as they went along. Ultimately, the adamant bacteria-squad agreed to close the refers up again so that we could prove that the food had been held at the required temperature the night before. To facilitate the test, an ominous call went out over thirty two-way radios, "Close all the refers and do not open them under any circumstances." Shortly, 15,000 hungry people emerged from the stadium. We were seriously outnumbered.

15,000 people cannot pile into somebody's Mustang and head for a fast-food joint. If we did not feed them, they would go hungry. They mostly went hungry. Lunch hour came and went, as the refers lowered their temperatures minute by unbearable minute; degree by excruciating degree. The refers were, after all, now parked right under the Nevada sun. We gazed helplessly at 30 lines of overheated, exasperated people who were holding empty, pristine, blindingly white paper plates in the afternoon sunlight—lines as far as the eye could see. There was nothing we could do except explain and reassure.

I borrowed Carl's big hat and rollerbladed around the lot like a crazy person, coaching the staff. "Explain what is happening. Tell them we will open as soon as possible. Direct them to the beverage stations. Don't say that the Health Department wants to make sure our food hasn't gone bad." Proactive communication was not most of our acquired staff's forte. Flustered and confused, most of them found shelter under the closest canopy.

Interesting that a city as hot as Las Vegas could be capable of such a cold shoulder. Maybe this right-to-work state was not as right-to-work as it would have us believe.

I found out the delicious news much later, back at the hotel and on my second Singapore Sling served in my purple plastic souvenir glass. Two buffet lines, 700 yards across the burning asphalt and oblivious to those thermometers of doom, had actually opened and served a record number of guests.

Michael Hollingsworth—a special events fixture in L.A. then and since—had faithfully managed his section exactly to plan. About 10 minutes prior to the arriving Feds, Michael's radio battery had very conveniently, but quite honestly, died. With our production Winnebago just a silver spec on the horizon, Michael had flung open his refer with abandon and never looked back. Captain of his ship, and quite oblivious to the storm, Michael plied his crew with encouragement, quenched them with bottled water, and lathered them in SPF 50 sunscreen. His fearless team feverishly grilled, tossed, and steamed within an inch of their lives, ultimately serving a record number of guests with nary a HazMat suit in sight. Michael will go down in history as the man who served 750 hamburgers to McDonald's, in an hour, in the desert sun, come what may. Nobody got sick.

Not to be outdone, apparently, Nancy Gulla, fully recovered from her vapors the day before and sporting an enviable Katherine Hepburn-style hat of her own, had also faithfully opened her hors d'oeuvres buffet with her team. Nancy's recovery and zeal may be a testament to the stimulating attributes of the two cute EMTs the day before.

"I don't want to lose the money!" Nancy had retorted to anyone who suggested that she possibly take the day off. I don't know what had happened to Nancy's radio, perhaps it was left on the seat of her refer or forgotten during her one trip to the portable that day. Nancy's team served Ambrosia's signature homemade guacamole and salsa, newly invented blue corn chips, and crudité with homemade dips (spinach and shrimp—Carl's own recipes) by the bucket.

Nancy's team ultimately ran out of every item—all the while marveling at the inordinate number of guests who were content eating just the hors d'oeuvres.

Award Season

IT'S NICE JUST TO BE NOMINATED

Off the back of their great success spearheading the Academy Awards® Governors Ball, Carl and David were hired again the following year. Ambrosia's lead coordinator didn't show up at meetings, so… there I was. I found myself walking through the hallowed halls of our client, the Academy of Motion Picture Arts and Sciences on Wilshire Boulevard. I strode past vintage movie posters, as well as more than a few glass-encased Oscars®. I longed to stop and reverently study each one. I was an actress at the Motion Picture Academy for the first time, so of course I was mesmerized and excited. Yes, I imagined we'd probably talk about catering at some point, too.

I was met by Otto Spoerri, Controller of the Academy, who organized the complex and the politically-charged Governors Ball seating plan, and Bruce Davis, the Executive Director of the Academy and very much the captain of the ship. For the second year, the Shrine Auditorium was chosen for the Oscar telecast, after which the Governors Ball for 1,700 guests would commence in the Shrine's Exhibition Hall. I arrived at the meeting.

"Who are you?" they asked, not impolitely. They had important work to do.

"I'm, Cheryl," I said, feeling perfectly at home, though maybe not for the reason they thought. Their expressions were blank for the moment. "I run the floor for Ambrosia," I continued.

"Oh. okay." They commenced firing off questions, a number of which I thought didn't have much to do with serving dinner, but they asked, so I answered.

"How do we improve guest flow? How do we ensure that guests sit at their assigned tables? How do we coordinate security protocols with all departments in the ballroom.

I was improvising, but my responses really made sense to me, and the Academy executives appeared to agree. Otto and Bruce sat back and considered me. Suddenly, I realized I was no longer as behind-the-scenes as before.

It was around this time that I had been producing an evening of six one-act plays at the Fountainhead Theater in Hollywood, with four acting friends, three of whom I had met through catering. They were all catering captains at the Oscars, too. We played for six nights over three weekends. The reviews were good. I invited everybody I had ever dealt with at the Academy, from the head honchos to the secretaries, to a performance. Eventually, then-Director of Communications, John Pavlik, sent out an inter-office memo about the show, possibly to stave off my persistent reminders. One Saturday in particular, about 40 Academy people showed up, Bruce included!

Yes! I decided. My catering days are numbered.

OPPOSITE PAGE
72nd Academy Awards®
Governors Ball Preview
From left:
Designer Douglas Johnson,
Academy of Motion Picture
Arts and Sciences President
Robert Rehme,
Wolfgang Puck's CEO and
President Carl Schuster,
Songwriter Alan Bergman,
Cheryl Cecchetto, Ball Chair
Sid Ganis and Mark's Garden
Florist Chris Thompson
©A.M.P.A.S.
Oscar Statuette ©A.M.P.A.S.®

Three days after our second successful ball, exhausted, happy (and did I mention exhausted?), I received a letter at my apartment. The envelope was embossed with the unmistakable raised gold lettering of the Academy of Motion Picture Arts and Sciences letterhead.

Dear Cheryl: Thank you for your organization skills and a spectacular evening.

Your efforts have not gone unnoticed.

How cool. I've been noticed by the Academy of Motion Picture Arts and Sciences. I'm not sure I read the rest. Catering was really not even my gig. Once again, my imagination soared.

Five months later, in August, I was called into the Academy's offices for an interview, this time by Otto, and the late Charlie Powell, the Ball Chair that year. Four months prior, my mother had been discovered to be terminally ill. She actually passed the day before my interview. I was arranging to fly home, when I phoned my sisters.

"I don't know why they want to see me," I told them. I was hoping that they wanted a little logistical help with a movie, or maybe there was a little acting part they needed filled. But now was not the time.

"Go to the interview Cheryl, then come," they advised.

"I don't want to go," I repeated. I felt particularly sad to be so far away from home at that moment.

But they insisted, "Mum would want you to go."

They were right. My father was also ailing at this time. I could just hear his voice saying, "Cheryl. We are okay. Go through the door."

The Academy knew nothing about my mother. I held myself together and went to my interview, eager to discover what they wanted. I glossed over the part about the Academy not actually producing movies. It is a non-profit organization that promotes the industry and manages a huge treasure trove of films and archives. They also hand out all the Academy Awards. They did offer me a job…

"Cheryl, we'd like you to manage the Governors Ball, all aspects, from our end."

"Oh." I thought carefully, then answered politely: "You know, I'm an actress, and this is somewhat of a sideways move for me. Let me think about it for a few days." I flew home. It was a challenging time for thinking.

Once again, my sisters counseled me," Cheryl, you have to do it. Just take the job and see what happens."

"But I won't be able to go to auditions," I mused, not that I went to very many.

Something else was knocking on my brain, as well. My mother had just passed at age 72—too young. I treasured my relationship with my parents, who were older than my peers' parents. I had always found their wisdom and unique perspective of the world fascinating. My father was now in a special-needs home in Toronto, four hours from everything he knew, having suffered a stroke. If I ever had children—which I absolutely intended to do—it was now quite likely that neither of my parents would ever meet them. What was the universe trying to tell me?

"You can always quit, Cheryl," my sister Corinne said. "Just open the door and see what happens."

That did it. The position was part-time, and seasonal. I certainly had enjoyed organizing the event from the standpoint of catering. Working for the Academy promised more comprehensive involvement, which intrigued me. I'd be working alongside various important and otherwise famous Hollywood people, which I had to admit appealed to me. Who knows, something wonderful might still happen in my acting career. I'm a bright girl, but I still didn't get it.

Something wonderful did happen.

In spite of my actress self, as I continued to garner more scope and responsibilities in special events, I was experiencing deeper investment, fulfillment, and passion in my work. I enjoyed nurturing ideas, driving them and witnessing them coming to fruition. Even Las Vegas, though a nightmare, I'd found exhilarating, with so many people looking to me for support and solutions and with so much at stake. This is what it felt like to be at the helm of my own life, not at the mercy of Hollywood. This worked. Over the course of the first four years working for the Academy, I realized that I wasn't an actress. I had incidentally found my true passion: special events.

My new journey began, and I was soon to meet some of the most talented people in the business, to name a few: Jeff Williams of Classic (Regal) Rents, Lonnie Eggleston of Unique Party Rentals, Roberta Karsch of Resource One, Mark Held of Mark's Gardens, and Sharon Sacks of Sacks Productions, all soon to become good friends. It was during this time that I started my business in earnest from my garage, with Dennis Lumpkin, Rebecca Barash (now Withey) and MaryJane Velasko (now Partlow). We were off and running. Looking back, I realize now that luck doesn't really just show up. I realize that work ethic gives birth to luck. I figured out what it was that I was looking for, because of the searching. While working diligently toward a goal, I was sideswiped by my actual destiny.

Carl Bendix's Guacamole and Torte

This is my favorite quick and easy guacamole dip but if you would like to keep going, you'll end up with Carl's amazing guacamole torte.

INGREDIENTS

Guacamole

5 avocados

2 oz. (60 g) chopped cilantro

2 Roma tomatoes, diced

¼ white onion, diced

1 jalapeño, seeded and diced

½ a lime

Kosher salt, to taste

Refried beans

12 oz. (350 g) pinto beans (canned)

1 white onion, diced

¼ teaspoon cumin

½ teaspoon paprika

¼ teaspoon chili powder

Kosher salt to taste

Oil of choice for refrying beans

Additional Torte ingredients needed

2 cups of shredded white cheddar cheese

2–3 cups sour cream

Red, yellow, & blue corn tortilla strips for decoration

Yellow, green, & red bell peppers for decoration

MAKES 1 TORTE

METHOD

For the guacamole

1. Skin and deseed avocados into a bowl. Add cilantro, tomato, onion, jalapeño, salt, and lime juice. Mash all ingredients together in bowl until smooth.

For the refried beans

1. To refry the beans you will need a medium sized pan on the stove with medium heat. Sauté chopped onion in oil until brown. Add cumin, paprika, chili powder, salt and beans, and stir. Continue stirring until beans appear refried; look somewhat dry but still moist.

For the torte

1. Cover the inside of a nine-inch spring form pan with plastic wrap.
2. Add refried beans to the spring form pan. Evenly distribute beans on bottom; should yield 1 inch layer of refried beans. Make sure to pack beans tightly. Allow refried beans to cool down in fridge for about 1–2 hours until beans are cold.
3. Add the guacamole on top of the beans until a smooth layer is achieved. Place the spring form pan into the fridge for about an hour to cool and harden. Then add white cheddar cheese on top of the guacamole and distribute it evenly. Place the spring form pan into the fridge for about an hour to cool and harden.
4. Take out the spring form pan and flip onto a flat surface and remove the plastic wrap along with the pan. Add sour cream on top of beans and evenly distribute all around. Serve with corn and flour tortilla chips. Optional decoration: Add the tortilla chips around torte, wedges of bell pepper on top of torte, and draw flowers on top of torte with sour cream.

Recipe courtesy of Armando Zavala

CHAPTER 4

I Gotta Be Me

Because I Say So

MY COMPANY, MY RULES

It's actually quite crowded "at the top". There are numerous, excellent special event producers in Los Angeles, many of whom are dear friends of mine, and countless others elsewhere. I am about to give you 29 possibly whimsical reasons why I started my own company. Yes, sometimes life just evolves. One situation presents an opportunity, morphing into another situation. At some point comes the "Aha moment". The decision to start my business was not so whimsical, and Easy Street was not one of the reasons.

At the age of four, I had already decided that I didn't need parents and that I was going to raise myself. At five, I had the audacity to tell them so. We all need parents, but I'm clear about where five-year-old me was coming from. I knew how I was wired. I had always intended and strived to be my own boss, to do my own thing, rather than rely on someone else.

I enjoy building a great team and empowering them to provide supreme service. Our clients share a common commitment to creative excellence. I'm thrilled to experience my own ideas realized, in the flesh. I also insist on finding the fun along the way, because I'm the boss, and I say so.

Running one's own company affords you the ability to run your life your own way, to do what you need to do, go where you need to go. The other side of the coin: work weeks may turn into 24/7, especially when approaching large events, because if something goes wrong or requires a decision, you need to be there. Sure, the compliments are welcome, but the boss needs to take the hits, too. The buck really does stop here. Bottom line, I'm happiest in the trenches with everyone else.

Sequoia Vice President Gary Levitt—my unbelievably dedicated partner (in crime) for 12 years running—is my rock, my support, and my kindred spirit, and I am his. Much of my excitement for tackling the next project and confidence for success is the reassurance that Gary and I are at each other's side.

It's my company, my rules, my blood, sweat, and tears. Here are the 29 reasons I get up in the morning, besides hugging my kids:

PAGE 70
Pavel Kounine Photography

OPPOSITE PAGE
Left: Television Academy®
Hall of Fame with Rebecca
Barash (left) and Dennis
Lumpkin (center)
Craig Mathew
©ATAS/NATAS
Middle: Team photo at
Glen Ivy Springs
Right: In production mode

1. The opportunity to lead
2. The joy of mentoring
3. Empower people
4. Make a difference in your own backyard
5. Make a difference globally
6. Choose my own hours
7. Collaborate and create with an office of great people
8. Inspire a creative company culture
9. Take a chance
10. Inspire an altered state
11. Celebrate my clients' accomplishments and milestones
12. Leave behind great memories
13. Encourage laughter
14. Debate
15. Manifest spectacular experiences
16. Communicate through all of the senses
17. Spark romance in everything
18. Inspire others to celebrate
19. Bring people together
20. Share ideas
21. Develop and introduce new talent
22. Discover new design, style, and tastes
23. Entice anticipation
24. Intrigue and pamper
25. Express passion
26. Be of service
27. Give back
28. Develop strategic life plan
29. Open a bottle of wine after work with my staff if I feel like it

Whose Idea Was This Anyway?

THE WONDERFUL WORLD OF A.D.D.

As the orchestra approaches its crescendo, the celebration we have spent months conceiving, nurturing and perfecting is drawing to a close. Phew! I feel a number of emotions. First and foremost being—boy, am I exhausted!

In the final weeks preparing and then ultimately managing a full-scale event, we don't fully allow ourselves to feel as tired as we are. The show must go on and all that. After the final curtain, the hours of sleep and number of yoga classes I've missed can really hit home. When my head hits the pillow at night, I am sleeping in less then two minutes (Bliss!). But more than fatigue, there is a sense of lightness, relief and profound achievement, as well as one of gratitude and affection for the devoted colleagues who've contributed to a great success.

We did it! Time for a little celebration of our own. Somebody find me a glass of champagne. Wait, find everyone a glass of champagne. I personally hand out the bubbly to my staff and crew until everyone on the team is holding a flute. As the last guests trickle out, we sit at several re-set tables in a corner of our beautiful room. This is our opportunity to enjoy our creation with absolutely no obligation to do anything, except, well… enjoy it. Sometimes our clients will join us too. These hard-working guys and gals have wolfed down their share of pizza, protein bars, and Red Bulls in the past week, and so have I—working into the wee hours to get everything just right. Believe me, I'm right there with them.

As we toast each other, certain elements of the décor may already be disassembling around us. The venue, anxious to reclaim the space for their next event, provides only a couple of days to deconstruct the set. Even as chandeliers are being lowered, or the dance floor is disappearing piece by piece, the warm tone of togetherness lingers. I love visiting all the staff tables, and one by one we recount our most memorable moments: the craziest time, the closest call, or the biggest Achilles heal blister.

We celebrate our creation into the wee hours, way past my bedtime… but my mind is already spinning. "Hmmmm. Next year…"

A large-scale production may require a year of imagining, coordinating, constructing, and detailing in order to finally achieve fruition. Though I definitely spend a few days after the Governors Ball decompressing and relaxing with my family, it's also true that the morning after the Ball I wake up nervous… and excited about next year. Assuming that we are hired again next year, we are expected to once again outdo ourselves. The best way I know to overcome trepidation or the unknown is to spring into action.

Before my first cup of tea the morning after the show, ideas are already knocking around in my brain. I don't mind; I welcome them and more importantly, I trust them. The possibilities can be very right brained, or out

OPPOSITE PAGE

84th Academy Awards®

Governors Ball

Line 8 Photography

Oscar Statuette ©A.M.P.A.S.®

PAGE 76-77

Design concepts to completion

Nadine Froger Photography

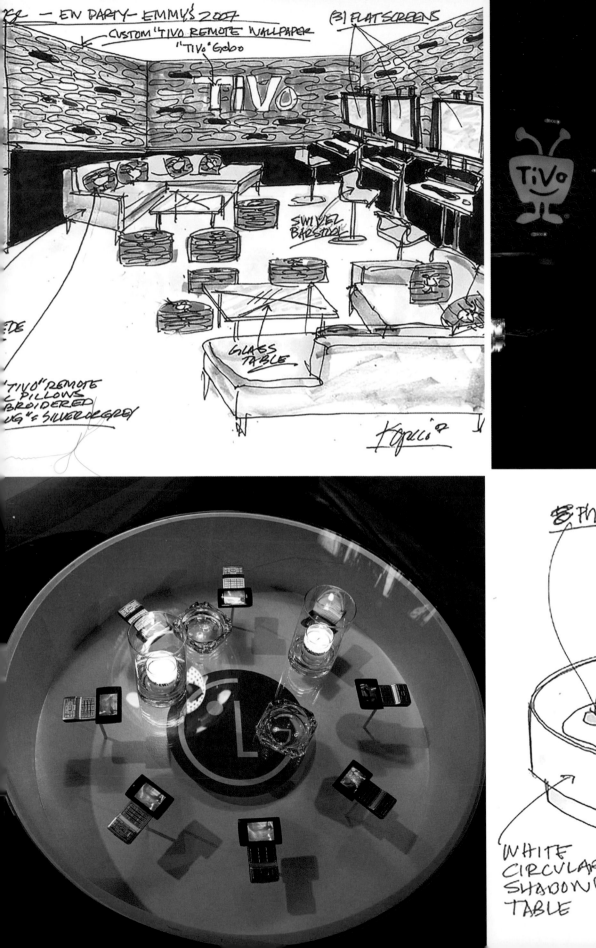

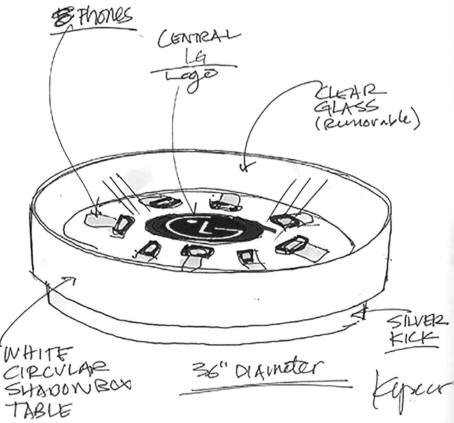

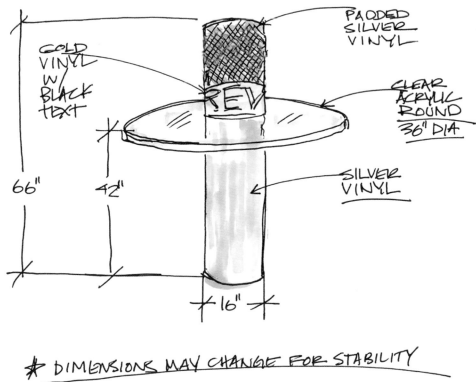

GOLD VINYL W BLACK TEXT

PADDED SILVER VINYL

CLEAR ACRYLIC ROUND 36" DIA

SILVER VINYL

REV

66"

42"

16"

✱ DIMENSIONS MAY CHANGE FOR STABILITY

Kyneo '07

of left field. Strange, those terms pretty much describe the same thing. For a while scientists hypothesized that the left sides of our brains handled reason, mathematics, and "pants-before-shoes" sorts of decisions, while the right brain harbored our emotions, creativity, and whimsy. Even though scientists are now reneging on that cerebral arrangement, creative people are still labeled, "right-brained". I never know where or when the muses will come knocking, but when they do, I listen. I can't really take responsibility for them. I just take copious notes. On the surface, some ideas may seem goofy, unlikely, or even impossible. But I don't judge.

Feng Shui, the science of spatial balance and energy, guides me through all of my event planning. Hollywood events are often historical in nature, therefore classic design, architecture and golden-era Hollywood chic frequently commingle with the most cutting-edge design and technology.

While my inspiration comes from many sources, I'm tactile, so rather than surf the web, I prefer the weight of a book in my hand; I need the feel of the glossy, full-sized photographs on my fingers and the reassurance of my scribbled Post-it notes. I like the fragrance of bound pages. I'm intoxicated by bookstores. I'll sometimes sneak into a library, forget where I am, forget the time, and suddenly it's four hours later. One of my favorite books is *The Grand Literary Cafés of Europe*. There are clues everywhere in this book; either the interior design of a small coffee shop, the detailing of the china, or the lace fringe of a tablecloth, all provide food for thought. The books on my shelves at home chronicle the many, seminal Hollywood theaters and clubs of the past, such as El Mocambo, the Rainbow Room, the Cocoanut Grove, and the grand El Capitan Theatre.

Magazines such as *Los Angeles*, *Savoir*, *Home and Garden*, and *Condé Nast* occupy my coffee table. They're not intended as showpieces. The magazines in my living room are plastered with Post-it notes protruding from the pages. Sometimes it's not the main focus of a magazine article that inspires, but the environs in which it is set, such as a cobblestone street or the bougainvillea hanging over an awning.

Many of the great artists and designers, past and present, influence me deeply. Reading about them and marveling at their images help me recharge; they're my mini vacation. I am excited by the pioneering designs of Dorothy Draper and the explosive impact of Art Deco, born of the works of Picasso and Tamara de Lempicka, as well as the unrivaled film and theater sets of Tony Duquette. The creativity of florist Daniël Ost is a revelation, as is the art and fashion of designer Elsa Schiaparelli. The famed Los Angeles-centric architect, Paul R. Williams, and his Saks Fifth Avenue Streamline Moderne building was the inspiration for the 2010 Academy Awards® Governors Ball ceiling. I've even had the opportunity to work with a few of these great artists; collaborating with the revolutionary Hiro Yamagata for the 1997 Academy Awards Governors Ball and Dale Chihuly in 1998. Sometimes, I have to pinch myself. The brilliantly eccentric Keith Greco designed many of the diverse elements of our Entertainment Weekly's Pre-Emmy® Party in 2007. I remember how once we had to scramble to find Keith a pair of slacks when he showed up for a design meeting at the Beverly Hills Country Club dressed in jeans and a T-shirt. Oddly, Keith's dreadlocks down to his ankles passed the club's General Manager's inspection, but his stone-washed jeans had to go. I love creative people.

Creative hints show up from all directions. Important sources include not just publications, but incidental local excursions and wider travel, not intentionally having anything to do with my job. My philosophy, for starters, as far as creativity is concerned, is to is to put my iPhone and tablet in a drawer, relax my shoulders,

get outside and look up. I find inspiration everywhere: at dress shops, fabric shops, music, the theater and architecture. Even Los Angeles is a haven for inspiring architecture, though you sometimes have to look for it. Seek out a Frank Lloyd Wright home, the Walt Disney Concert Hall, or the Griffith Observatory if you need convincing.

As well as sights, it's smells, sounds, tastes and textures that also inspire me. I have enjoyed (usually with my children) wonderful exhibits at the museums closest to me—MOCA (the Museum of Contemporary Art) and LACMA (the Los Angeles County Museum of Art). Fascinating exhibits often travel though the larger museums, such as the King Tut exhibit from several years ago. They're such a gift. We've marveled at temporary exhibits of the work of the Impressionists, the stunning *Calla Lilies of Diego Rivera*, Andy Warhol's larger than life *Campbell's Soup Cans*, and the playfully dark mind of Tim Burton. It's no wonder that children's museums and zoos have caught onto featuring sections where the kids can enjoy a hands-on, tactile experience via science experiments and meeting some of the animals close up. MOCA had a great graphic artist exhibit a few years ago. My kids, especially my son, Milan, loved it. The comprehensive stimulation of all the five senses is also key to the ideal special event experience.

My vegan daughter, Mia, has introduced us to some absolutely amazing cuisine, born of the reality that serious innovation and imagination is required to create delicious recipes without animal products. Delicious they are. Then there's my son, who brings me right back down to earth when he begs me to take him out for a meatball sandwich at his favorite, Ma and Pa Italian restaurant.

On a Friday night, my family and I sometimes join dear friends for dinner at their home, and I'll come across a modern art painting or an intriguing chair in the corner that sets off an idea. I also enjoy exploring new restaurants, book fairs, and farmers markets. I'm not usually thinking, I'd better go to that flea market for some décor ideas. Any creative person, any person, must get out and live life because ultimately, that is what inspires our creativity. American writer Kurt Vonnegut says we are all artists, or that we definitely should be.

My family has had the good fortune to return to the bustle of New York and enjoy its theaters and museums. Last year, I fulfilled a lifelong dream of visiting my cultural *alma mater*, Italy, with my family. I hadn't seen Italy since my thirties. Inspiration abounds in Italy: the paintings, sculpture, architecture, music, corner store windows and the classic fashion and flair of Italian women. Of course, we ate the food. Oh, the food! True to my cultural heritage, familial celebration always moves me, even visiting elderly cousins of my father whom I have never met before.

I recently rendezvoused in Las Vegas with my uber-talented girlfriend and designer, Gail Taylor. In addition to enjoying a much needed girls weekend, Gail and I explored the wildly creative lobbies and architecture on the Strip, such as at hotels Paris Las Vegas and The Venetian. Las Vegas design and visual innovation is often way over the top, and intentionally so. The design choices are bold, playful, and definitely innovative. Clues are everywhere.

At the Bellagio Hotel, we smiled as we walked under the massive Dale Chihuly glass sculpture in the lobby. We had worked with Chihuly at the Academy Awards Governors Ball at the Dorothy Chandler Pavilion in Los

OPPOSITE PAGE

81st Academy Awards®

Governors Ball

Line 8 Photography

PAGE 84

Warner Bros. *Friends*

Wrap Party

Nadine Froger Photography

PAGE 85

Emirates West Coast

Roadshow

Nadine Froger Photography

Angeles, where he constructed a dazzling glass pergola over the guest arrival area.

After dark, on Las Vegas Boulevard, Gail and I swayed gently along with the Bellagio's swirling, dancing musical fountain, and I was reminded once again of the timeless beauty and mesmerizing sound of moving water.

I'm always watching and listening, filing images and ideas in the back of my brain. As a project comes up, I fully consider the client's vision and mission statement and then call up those many muses of color, texture and shapes. I revisit all my Post-it notes. Soon, combinations of ideas begin to form. I research them further and a theme is born.

I often gravitate toward one of my favorite themes, classic and timeless old Hollywood. It is at once grand, luxurious, yet relaxing. One feels pampered even before being delivered one's first drink. Ideally, you might expect Fred Astaire, with Ginger Rogers in his arms, to glide through the room at any moment. At other times my instincts gravitate toward an architectural aesthetic, driven by strong shapes, clean lines, directed light and movement.

One December, at Vancouver International Airport, I walked under a striking tubular chandelier and stopped to enjoy it. I'm sure most of the rushing holiday passengers, forced to maneuver around me with their suitcases and gifts, wondered briefly why I was standing there in their way, looking up. Perhaps I motivated just a few to pause, take a breath and look upwards as well? I snapped a quick shot with my camera. The chore of changing planes can have its advantages; that chandelier inspired the décor theme for an entire event.

I think my function is to introduce unlikely styles and archetypes to each other, thus creating a not-before-seen dynamic. Some of the best ideas are born of the synergy between tried-and-true methodology, newly introduced.

In 2008, an economic crisis emerged that caused more than some concern for many people around the world. A grand, conspicuous Ball designed for the 2009 Oscars would not reflect the mood of an audience just becoming acquainted with the word austerity. As I searched for the right feel to resonate with the prevailing reality, I discovered an article featuring a classic teahouse in Beijing. Suddenly I realized the elegant and minimalist Asian style would create a sense of pause, peace and reflection during an otherwise very turbulent 2009. Thus, the annual Academy Awards Governors Ball evolved into a reflective, refined, yet stunning Asian fusion, East meets West theme. We amplified the elegant simplicity of the Zen-like teahouse with images of a rock garden, projected onto clean, modern architectural shapes. It was tasteful, sublime, and so beautiful.

Even as my musings spin around me, I remind myself that there are obvious clues from the client that I mustn't miss. Perhaps the celebration is private, familial and personal? Or, for corporate clients, what is the corporate culture? What is their vision, and how do they describe the thrust or purpose of their event? I'll always ask, what do you want the world to say about you and your organization? I must consider the season, as well as how the aesthetic of the venue lends itself to the whole occasion. If the location is fixed, then the theme or charm of the space must reflect and support the art direction of the project, and vice versa.

I launch ideas very early, sharing and building upon them with my staff and vendors. I surround myself with talented and trusted artisans, technicians and designers of every discipline; people who know the technical side of things, who know where to procure specific materials, and who are just as excited about taking my

ideas and running with them to create something completely new.

My initial inspiration is very lateral, ideas coming at me from all angles; dots that need connecting. These ideas evolve through collaboration; attention turns to practicality, from concept to production. All the while, we keep in mind our standards and the expectations of discerning clients. All of my clients have exquisite taste, so it is all the more challenging and satisfying to realize their vision. Annual, recurring events are particularly exciting because after the previous year's success, the obligation and opportunity to surpass and surprise is palpable. It does not escape me that we are very fortunate to be able to create fresh, memorable experiences together, year after year.

OPPOSITE PAGE
Surprise 50th Birthday
Line 8 Photography

PAGE 92
57th Primetime Emmys®
Governors Ball Rendering

PAGE 93
57th Primetime Emmys®
Governors Ball
Nadine Froger Photography

Five Minutes, Ms. Cecchetto

THE LIMELIGHT

The word "limelight" was coined to name a process discovered by a gentleman named Goldsworthy Gurney back in 1820. It involved subjecting a piece of lime to a sizzling hot flame of hydrogen and oxygen. The result was a brilliant white light. The effect was first used in 1837 in a theater in Covent Garden, London, in order to enhance the actor's presence on stage. The figure of speech has lingered ever since.

Today, "limelight" encompasses the often aggressive media exposure surrounding celebrities. Publicity focuses on their projects and their way of life; their relationships, their lavish houses and cars, the limousines, the red carpet, as well as "who they are wearing."

In my line of work, the media offers me the opportunity to spark interest in a celebration, to entice invited guests, and to quench the thirst of a public audience who "want the details". In a party town such as Los Angeles, publicity is an essential element to a special event's success. Publicity draws guests and a curious public to the celebration, to a rarefied environment that will affirm cherished relationships and accomplishments, while fostering new partnerships at the same time. These opportunities abound within a carefully crafted atmosphere of entertainment, pampering, and sheer fun. In fact, the most successful event is experienced as spontaneous and organic, with all the producing parties essentially disappearing into the ether. A special event emulates a live performance. In that analogy, my role is decidedly "back-stage".

Not everyone is messengered a VIP pass to hot-ticket, Hollywood celebrations. The next best thing for big and small screen Hollywood enthusiasts is an insider interview and behind-the-scene sneak-peeks, when we roll back the curtain and reveal a few delicious details or trivia that might not otherwise be available to those on the other side of the velvet rope. In my world, television, social media and magazine spreads are essential opportunities to "tell the tale".

The public wants to know what Wolfgang Puck, Joachim Splichal, or Curtis Stone may have up their sleeves for the evening's signature hors d'oeuvre, or custom dessert. What top-tier wines, champagne, and signature cocktail can we share (and recommend)? What about the entertainment? Is Tony Bennett performing? John Legend? What theme is the décor, and so on. I love sharing all the details we've worked on so diligently.

Speaking on behalf of events constitutes a double-edged sword, especially if your clients have worldwide reputations and valued brands. Truthfully, I'm not always able to answer everything asked of me. Some information is privileged or considered high security. Interviewers often innocently press for answers that would reveal sensitive information. Sidestepping some questions requires all the tact and grace I can muster. I just smile, evade the question, and share what excites me about the project.

Doesn't everyone love talking about their hobby with anyone who will listen, just as I felt proud to be pulled out of bed to play the accordion for my parents and their friends so many years ago. Half the time, if I'm in the midst of production, I may be wearing jeans and a sweatshirt, with no make-up, and have been working beyond my twelfth hour on the job that day. In truth, I've discovered that none of this matters when I am sharing something I love. I've learned how to hold my own on camera, though it hasn't always been that way. I still laugh (and cringe) when I remember my first occasion addressing an audience while holding a microphone.

Hailing back to my early days as an actress in Los Angeles, I was a bit of a Lucille Ball type, stubborn but well-meaning, quirky, and pretty darn funny. I love talking with people, and I loooove entertaining. I even auditioned once to play Lucy on Broadway.

One day (don't ask me how), I auditioned and was hired to "warm up" a sitcom audience for the taping of a new, half-hour show, *The Pursuit of Happiness*, starring Patty Duke. On the surface, the job was simple. As the audience filed into their seats, I would interact, amuse them, tell jokes, point out weird outfits, invite them to tell jokes—basically focus them on the task at hand and "warm them up" for the show. That's not the whole job. Once a taping is underway, the warm-up host must entertain the audience between the takes, during scene and costume changes, and so on. Sitcom tapings can last three hours or more, and involve shooting every scene two or three times, plus retakes and pick-ups. Warming up a sitcom audience is a unique, learned skill, so I discovered.

So, I'm standing in front of the audience seating, with my microphone, in the relative dark, waiting for my intro. The audience is filing in, and then it hits me: terror, the sinking feeling that in one minute I'm going to be the center of attention, one thousand eyes on me, no lines memorized, no rehearsal. I've never warmed up an audience before. That's the caveat I never mentioned to anyone during my audition. Gulp. My heart starts playing jump rope with my throat. My legs suddenly feel like we've never been introduced. I lose the feeling in my lips… and the whole room is moooooving in slooooow moooootion.

My intro blares over the house speakers. I hear my name announced very excitedly, as if I'm about to perform some death-defying feat, as opposed to just die, and the spotlight rushes over to find me. This is the weird part— before the light reaches me, I lay down on the floor. Or, perhaps I realize I'm lying on the floor, but I'm not sure how I got there. It's a blur. This is one of those out-of-body experiences I've heard tell about, I think to myself, or maybe I'm just wishing that this wasn't my body at this particular moment. Oh yes… I lay down on the floor. Face up… eyes closed… praying, praying this is all a bad dream, hoping I will wake up in my bed.

When I open my eyes, I see the spotlight pass over me, now dancing all over the sound stage, much like the searchlight at a prison, it seems to me. I notice that my face is perhaps five inches from the feet of the first row of the audience. VIPs and friends of the cast sit in the first row, their seats taped over beforehand, displaying their VIP names in foreboding magic marker. The VIPs stare at me, as bewildered as I'm sure I appear to them. The spotlight is bouncing around the room with increasingly frantic determination.

The voice over the house speakers announces me again, as intent on introducing me as I am intent on not being introduced. I heard you the first time, I'm thinking to myself. HOW does announcing my name a second time change the situation?

I'm going to wake up now. Okay, now. Okay, now. I don't wake up. I decide to be brave, to "walk through the open door". I stand up, the spot hits me head on, and I begin to speak into the microphone. Instead of words, I hear an interesting language devoid of consonants, and definitely not English. I can't feel my lips.

"Flapb flab floonb floob."

No one laughs. In fact, the crowd grows silent. I feel the sweat trickling down my neck, or am I melting? I have to do something, and fast. I decide to lay down again. I'm not sure who is making these decisions. Once again on the floor, I pray to be somewhere else. I look up again at the people in the first row, this time at someone who looks a lot like Patty Duke. Was it her sister, perhaps? I say simply, "Can I be you?"

The crowd is stunned. The silence roars. I can't think of anything funny, not even that the situation might be remotely funny anytime later in life. In a primal fit of fight or flight, I bolt for the restroom. Once there, I want to throw up. I am paranoid that two burly stagehands will come for me and force me onto the stage. I find myself sticking a leg out the bathroom window, like some thief in the night. Yes, I am trying to climb out the bathroom window. Lucille Ball would have been proud. If I wasn't already humiliated, I am humiliated now. Yes, I am definitely humiliated.

Somehow, reason returns and I decide to climb back inside and go out to face the music, at least apologize —but do so nowhere near the reach of the searchlight or the mic. However, as I arrive at the stage, the taping has already begun, no doubt to cover up my debacle.

I actually have no idea how they covered that night, without a warm-up person. Perhaps a producer or assistant-stage manager filled in. I was fired, of course. A seminal moment in my life, I would never be the same after that gig. Hours later that night, after much soul searching, tossing and turning, I did discover the secret to staying loose and alive on camera. Never get caught up in your own story. Be interested, not interesting. Get the focus off yourself. Don't seek attention, give it, and above all, "tell the tale".

Oh yes, if you're feeling all alone when the limelight comes after you, definitely don't lay down. It's even lonelier down on the carpet.

LEFT
Rehearsing script with
Jacki Weaver (2nd from left)
at the 9th Annual G'DAY
USA Black Tie Gala
Barbara Green

Is This Thing On?

I've had the opportunity to speak throughout North America, Australia and the Philippines, with more dates on the horizon. Speaking about my passion evolved due to the fact that I began my career as a manager, evolved into a producer and subsequently an owner of a special event company. Through the years, these growing responsibilities have obliged me to also play the role of teacher and communicator. At the conclusion of my first few appearances, so many people approached me to ask, "When will you write a book?"

I've discovered that the process of sharing my world of special events involves storytelling. A necessary element of speaking is entertainment and fun. Speaking is akin to a stand-up comedy act, or more specifically a one-woman show: it has to be informative, personal and hopefully meaningful, while also entertaining, to ensure that the audience remains engaged.

Speaking engagements take me all over the world and I have become accustomed to receiving many requests. One of my most curious invitations was to speak in the Philippines. The request arrived at my office in a FedEx package and resembled a certificate, as if I had won a vacation of some sort, or purchased a lottery ticket for a Filipino timeshare. It was sent from an organization called MICE (Meetings, Incentives, Conventions and Exhibitions). Initially, I didn't fully understand what I was looking at and was confused by the flowery language, the many brochures and pamphlets, and the formality, as if I were some sort of dignitary. I considered that it might be a prank since requests to speak typically arrive via email. I actually asked my assistant, "Chelsea, is this for real?" We called the phone number in the Philippines to discover that it was indeed a legitimate request to appear.

My speaking engagements require basic non-negotiables. My contact, Jerome, who had sent the invite, was polite and gracious to a fault, yet completely steadfast in terms of the materials and logistics he would provide on his end. Despite all the negotiations, I was interested in and slightly anxious about the person I would be meeting upon arrival in the Philippines. Upon meeting Jerome, I discovered him to be even more gracious and appreciative than via email, and that he had a tremendous sense of humor. He was an absolute pleasure to work with.

At the farewell dinner, I stood up to thank the key organizers, expressing my original reservations about Jerome, with whom I had developed a real friendship. To my surprise, he stood and spoke of his initial reservations about me too! "Who was this woman, I wondered?" he said. "Would she make continuous, unreasonable demands?"

We were both well-meaning business people, coming from very different realities, but working toward the same goal. I eventually realized that Filipinos do not necessarily enjoy the resources that may be taken for granted elsewhere in the world. I realized that Jerome was firm in terms of the arrangements because they were all he could offer. In general terms, businesses in the Philippines do not have the same financial resources as we do in the U.S. and other first world countries.

As with stand-up comedy, public speaking is more about the audience than about the speaker. In my case, the audience is actually in search of themselves within the world of special events, essentially searching for that unique product or potential enticement that they could offer to attract business and be successful. Before I prepare for an appearance, I always research ahead of time and ask what the organization is all about. What is its mission statement? I'll check their website, Facebook page, and all of their social media. I'll ask the educational committee or conference planner of that group for insight into the specific goal of the conference. Based on what I learn, and their response, I present a synopsis of the presentation I'm planning. I include a basic theme and bullet points to be covered, depending on the goals of the business and the thrust of the convention or gathering. These points may include inspiration, motivation, work ethic, building a team, sales, service, while also detailing and including images of many of the events that my company has produced over the years. I then offer two to four sentences on each topic.

As a side note, I once asked a new client what the mission statement of their company was. Board members looked around the table at each other, and one finally answered, "That's a very good question." It's a very good question for any company, endeavor, or individual striving for success. I know that I earned my keep that day.

As I took to the stage in Davao, the Philippines, I told the audience right up front, "I talk fast at the best of times and I'll probably get a little excited as we get into this. So, if I'm speaking too quickly, somebody please raise your hand and ask me to slow down."

I was well into my second or third PowerPoint image, when I realized that, besides the sound of my own voice, I could hear a pin drop.

What an attentive group. I'm doing well today, I thought to myself... Then, oh, wait a minute... "Okay, everyone who thinks I'm talking too fast, raise their hands?" A timid hand went up, then another, then a sea of hands. "All right, so we've established that you are very polite!"

The most enjoyable part of a presentation is the question and answer section, because it's the best opportunity to give the specific knowledge the audience is looking for. It's actually imperative that I listen to the audience throughout, sensing where their attention and interests lie. At the Philippines event, as at most presentations, there are standard questions I expect to be asked, such as, "What is going on in Hollywood?" It's fun to answer that one.

Other frequently asked questions include, "How can we create our own captivating and innovative special events?" or "What is the secret formula to your success?"

My answer: "There is no secret formula, beyond clear goals, consistent effort, and keeping your eyes and ears open. In lieu of a formula, lets talk about the process of discovery, resourcefulness, ingenuity, courage, and about partnerships with other creative people," and so we did.

My Filipino audience asked me very specifically, "How do we attract business, investment, and tourism based on who we are and our limited resources? What can we sell?"

I answered, "Actually, you already know the answer to that. You should find whoever came up with the catchphrase, 'It's more fun in the Philippines' and thank them. What I've discovered since arriving a few days ago is that you are fun, and that your open-heartedness and generosity is what you should sell. Plus your country is in the tropics, and very beautiful."

Another question, on a more personal note, was from a woman who stood to ask, bravely, "I was just fired and I don't know what to do. Why didn't my boss like me?"

I said, "Well, you are the bravest person in the room, standing up in front of hundreds of people asking this most personal and vital of questions." I continued, "Your boss not liking you is the least of your problems. If he was ungrateful or unreasonable or a tyrant, there's nothing you can do about that. But ask yourself: Did you add to the culture your boss was trying to create? Were you making your company money? Was this job the right match for you? Were you good at it?"

I then said, "Now that you no longer work for him, ask yourself: What is your ideal job description?" I counseled her to write out her perfect job, not just one she'd enjoy having, but one that would excite her, and at which she would excel.

I believe the greatest value in public speaking is the two-way, face-to-face, human exchange of ideas and good will. Special events do not exist for their own sake. The creativity, the grand scale, and the event itself is conceived to forge new relationships under the banner of a common goal. The nature and spirit of my business is inclusion and human synergy. In all my travels—not only at speaking engagements—I have discovered wonderful, common denominators among people, in addition to their generous hospitality. I notice that people of every culture are striving for the same goals everywhere I go: happiness, adventure, freedom to pursue their dreams, and the ability to give back. We especially share an intrinsic need to connect and of course, to celebrate together.

RIGHT
Warm welcome at
Philippines' M.I.C.E.
Conference

OPPOSITE PAGE
Keynote speaker at
Philippines' M.I.C.E.
Conference

Cheryl's Cioppino
(although my sister Carol thinks it's hers...)

INGREDIENTS

Tomato sauce

¾ cup (6 fl oz/175 ml) olive oil

2 tablespoons butter

1 green onion (scallion/spring onion) (including the top), finely chopped

3 green bell peppers (capsicum), seeded and diced

1 bunch Italian parsley, chopped

4–6 large garlic cloves, crushed

1 cup (8 fl oz/250 ml) canned tomato purée

2 x 14 oz (400 g) cans puréed tomatoes

2 cups (16 fl oz/500 ml) dry white wine

1 cup (8 fl oz/250 ml) water

1 cup (8 fl oz/250 ml) clam juice

4 bay leaves

1 teaspoon fresh rosemary, chopped

1 teaspoon fresh thyme, chopped

2 tablespoons sugar

½ teaspoon red chili flakes

1 tablespoon fresh basil, chopped

Salt and pepper, to taste

Seafood

20 mussels, cleaned

20 clams, cleaned

2 cups cut-up squid

1 lb (450 g) monk fish, cut into 1 in. (2.5 cm) chunks

20 large scallops

1 lb (450 g) cooked King Crab legs, cut into 1 in. (2.5 cm) chunks

20 large raw shrimp (prawns), tails on

SERVES 12–16

METHOD

For the tomato sauce

1. In a large pan, heat the olive oil and butter over medium heat until foaming. Add the onion, peppers and parsley and sauté for 20 minutes.

2. Add the remaining sauce ingredients. Bring to the boil, reduce the heat, and simmer for 1 hour.

3. Leave to cool. Cover and refrigerate overnight.

For the seafood

1. Slowly bring the tomato sauce to the boil. When boiling, add the mussels and clams and cook for 10 minutes.

2. Add the squid, monk fish, and scallops and continue cooking for 5–7 minutes.

3. Add the crab and shrimp and cook for 5 minutes, watching carefully to avoid overcooking (and keep shellfish from becoming tough).

4. Remove and discard any mussels and clams that don't open.

5. Serve immediately over Italian Polenta (see page 242).

CHAPTER 5

Divas, Disasters, and Near Misses

Hollywood North

CANUCKS

In 2001, I received a phone call out of the blue, "Cheryl Cecchetto? It's Perry Dellelce. We met on a playground when we were 10..."

" Okay," I replied.

"...and have not seen a whole lot of each other since." That second part I knew was true.

"Cheryl, I hear you're a big shot event producer in Hollywood now," he continued.

" Okay..."

"Well, I'm getting married and I'd like you to organize my wedding in Sudbury for 650 guests," he said. Had I heard that right?

"In Sudbury? My Sudbury? Canada?" I questioned. I knew there was also a Sudbury in Massachusetts, or perhaps Maine?

"Yeah," Perry replied. "Let's bring some of that Hollywood pizzazz up to The Great White North."

" Okay," I said, "It's so great that you got in touch. I don't remember the playground, but let me get back to you on this."

I called my sisters, who knew of Perry Dellelce. They remembered him from our childhood, and everyone up in Sudbury who knew him, knew he was now a big shot lawyer in Toronto. Eventually I discovered he was the nicest guy in the world, and also one of the most fun.

Remember Sudbury? It's 300 miles north of Toronto, accessible by a lone, usually-under-construction two-lane highway over hill and through dale, boasting frequent "Deer Crossing" and "Beware of Hunters" signs. I loved and still love Sudbury. Most of my huge, extended family lives there still. How fun would a pilgrimage home be, with my fledgling company and "Angeleno" compadres in tow? I envisioned nieces passing hors d'oeuvres, nephews bussing tables, and my sisters cooking amongst the chefs in the kitchen. But what L.A. producer in her right mind would consider tackling a décor and entertainment-driven event 'up north' for 650 guests, especially for a client throwing around words like "Hollywood pizzazz"? But the entire prospect was too enticing and romantic to say no. Sudbury would never know what hit them. I would never know what hit me. I was decidedly not in my right mind when I called back and said, "Let's do this."

In Sudbury, when I was young, a lodge full of Masons eating roast beef and mashed potatoes on card tables under fluorescent lights would be considered catering, with deviled eggs likely indicated. Yes, I love deviled eggs too, but I don't believe I had even seen a deviled egg in Los Angeles (since then, they've become trendy again). 10 years after moving away from Sudbury, I had no idea what to expect in terms of event facilities and infrastructure.

PAGE 104
63rd Primetime Emmys®
Governors Ball
"Bubble Girl" Performer
Nadine Froger Photography
©ATAS/NATAS

The January prior to the wedding, I led an on-site inspection, much like military scouts who check out the terrain before the "invasion". The terrain was daunting. We visited every school gymnasium, Elks Lodge, and Mason Club. No Sudbury venue could accommodate the guest count. Have you ever watched the sport of curling, when you slide a 'rock' over ice towards other rocks, accompanied by four frantic people with brooms, until your rock hopefully knocks the opponents' rocks out of the way, and lands on the bulls eye? The sport of ice curling is the curious marriage of bocce ball (Italian lawn bowling), and sweeping the porch. In Sudbury, curling is almost as inevitable as every Canadian boy learning to skate and hold a hockey stick at the same time as he learns to walk. The sport requires a really big ice rink. One of Sudbury's largest buildings in 1994 was the ice rink, right next to the Idylwylde Golf Course.

Without them exactly understanding why, I dragged my advance team to the rink. In May, the rink would be mothballed into a deserted box with a concrete floor, until the following winter season. In our business, that's what is called a "raw space", teeming with curlers and their admirers, all in toques, and we could all see our breath. The owner didn't know they owned a raw space until I told him. I said, "I want to rent your rink for a formal sit-down dinner in May." I had to repeat myself. May represented the owner's free time, dedicated pretty much to golf and fishing. I convinced him, or perhaps Perry did.

The mixed blessing of a raw space is that you can create everything exactly to your vision and liking, but every item of equipment and staff must be hired in. That is a complex process and can be costly. I sat down with Pete from Pete's Rentals in Sudbury, and told him gravely, "Look into my eyes, Pete. The third weekend in May, I want to rent everything you have. All of it." In the event world, rental companies' inventories include various styles of chairs, tables, tablecloths, dishes and glassware, kitchen equipment, and so on.

I had an identical conversation with the local lighting company. The quantities of equipment still weren't enough. Enter my sister and fledgling event specialist, Celia, who commandeered more rentals and equipment from Higgins Rentals, a small company in Toronto. Rising to the task, Higgins found an 18-wheeler to load everything in. That did it. I assigned Celia as Canadian production coordinator for the entire job.

The enthusiastic Idylwylde chefs agreed to provide the dinner, but could not commit their resources to hors d'oeuvres as well. They agreed to work with a supervising chef, the revolutionary Stuart Raymond of South Africa, already internationally known, and for some unknown but wonderful reason, based in Northern Ontario. Stuart created a cutting edge menu.

I called my sister, Carol, a fantastic cook and left her a message. "Guess what, Carol? Stuart Raymond said yes to cooking dinner. You are in charge of hors d'oeuvres. Bye!" Carol called back and said yes too, and immediately set out to find the most inventive and exciting recipes she could. I set Carol loose, along with her ex-husband, Sam Bruno (also an amazing cook) and our cousin, Christina. Carol's menu started out with coconut beer-battered shrimp and crostini wrapped in prosciutto. She was clearly the perfect choice for the job.

My teenage nieces were already seasoned in special events, having traveled down to L.A. to assist with many of my projects, while also enjoying some respite from Canuck winters. They phoned and booked every one of their friends four months in advance.

"Just reserve the date," they instructed. "We'll explain what you are doing later, as soon as we figure it out.

But buy a white button down shirt. Bye!"

The equipment was materializing. The menu was simmering. The job roster was coming together.

Meanwhile, during the same weekend I had sent my stage manager south to Toronto to listen to every top band he could find. At 12:30 a.m. a phone ringing at the camp startled me out of a deep sleep. "Cheryl, listen." He held a phone up toward the stage in some Toronto hot spot that he had wandered into so I could hear. I was sold, and he hired this wonderful, local Toronto band on the spot, as they stepped off the stage for their break.

Subsequently, after months of organizing back in L.A., on a sunny Wednesday in May, I returned to Sudbury with my hand-picked Sequoia production team, the fabulous forces of Chelsea Corvarubias and MaryJane Partlow, to join forces with my local relatives and workers. My fledgling company had grown to produce the Academy Awards® Governors Ball for 15 years. A production of this size, however, always mandates additional staff. My L.A. contingent consisted mostly of talented freelancers—most of whom were my friends. But creative people are, well… creative. My coup d'état was all-around creative genius Gail Taylor, in charge of décor. Two top-flight, L.A. event coordinators, Canadians Lesley Kyle-Wilson, and Bert Hilkes, were on board to organize the masses of waiters, kitchen staff, technicians and entertainers. Larry Oberman, one of my L.A. lighting designers, flew up with us to organize the lighting. I say organize, rather than design, because we had no clue what lighting equipment would be available. I also enlisted Chris Thompson from Mark's Garden in Los Angeles, and connected him with a team from Sudbury's finest, Rosemary Florists. Okay, we were all set, right?

So, long after their regular clientele had hung up their skates and put away their brooms for the season, we descended upon the ice rink next to Idylwylde golf course.

On our first day of "load-in", the first 18-wheeler of equipment arrived. The driver stepped out of the cab

ABOVE
Idylwylde Curling Club
Ice Rink before installation

OPPOSITE PAGE
Idylwylde Curling Club
Ice Rink transformed

to open up the back of the trailer; equipment and potted trees precariously stacked to the roof and all the way back to the doors.

"There you go, lady. Sign here please," stated the driver.

"What do you mean, there you go, lady…? Where are all your guys to place this stuff?" He gave me the vacant look of a man who had already performed his duty and was on his way for a well-deserved brewski or two.

He said nonchalantly, "We just deliver," with an accompanying expression that asked, "what planet are you from?"

L.A. rental companies deliver, place and then assign on-site staff at the producer's (my) beck and call, to move, adjust and order more of this or that. Was I spoiled? Here was a truck loaded to the gills with nobody to unload it. I found myself calling every cousin I had in town, every high school chum I could find in the phone book.

"Hi, Diane, remember me? Cheryl. We went to high school together. Got any sons? And do you still have your Lockerby High yearbook?" I was after surnames. Meanwhile, brother-in-law Steve also corralled some hefty guy-friends from out of nowhere, and the truck was unloaded. Stoves, Chiavari chairs, china and a dance floor emerged, and most distributed to preliminary positions. I pillaged staff from the Holiday Inn, the Caruso Club (exactly what it sounds like), and my uncle Romano's family restaurant, and once again purchased many a drive-thru burger, taco and chicken leg, trolling for waiters.

Every newbie we hired was wowed by our emerging creation. They thought we were so cool, and saw "pizzazz" in us we didn't know we had. Whatever they lacked in experience, they more than made up for in sheer enthusiasm. At this point, rumors of a big to-do were spreading across town, probably due to the cousins and teenagers we had hired spilling the beans back at home. People I didn't know, and many who I did, would drive up and peek in through the big barn doors where the ice-grooming machine usually appeared, in order to see for themselves the room beginning to take shape. My sister Corinne's job was to amuse my one-year-old son and three-year-old daughter for the duration. I didn't see either for 22 hours at a time, but I didn't have a moment to feel guilty. I would feel guilty later.

A hodge-podge of lighting equipment began to appear from hither and thither over the course of two days, which we continued to set on the floor in a corner of the rink before the almighty Larry. He divined the emerging lighting design based completely on the rag tag equipment sporadically placed in front of him, which is 100 percent the opposite of standard protocol. Design, then install is the usual order of the day.

"Oh, Cheryl, see that? That's a par 60, 120 watt lamp, or something like that. Sooo… yes, your cake will be lit, as soon as they fix the man lift."

I called my buddy Jeff Williams from Regal Rents in L.A.

"Jeff! Wanna come up for a Canadian vacation? No? Oh. In that case, how do you put together a dance floor?" I counted, "It's… 46… 47… 48… 3 x 3 foot pieces, stacked outside in the mud."

"Cheryl, pick up a Torx, Bristol, or Clutch Head screwdriver."

"Okay. What do they look like, in case I come across one?" Jeff's description went completely over my head. I sent my nephew, Matt, to a hardware store.

"What do they look like?" Matt asked. "Ask. And drive fast…" I told him.

I told Perry, "We need portable restrooms for this guest count." Perry's father, Nick, a true Sudbury character whose business was construction, had put himself at our disposal.

"I'll take care of it," he said.

I envisioned a trailer, on wheels, replete with private stalls, warm running water, gentle elevator music playing, and bow tied attendants wiping the mirrors and refilling the paper towels. The next day there was a plastic, portable outhouse sitting outside the arena, also in the mud, exactly what you'd expect to see sitting next to an outdoor construction site. It was sky blue, indicating that it was handicap friendly, and big enough to accommodate even the largest of teamsters. It was not aesthetically friendly, hygienically friendly, or in any other way friendly.

"Nick, what's that over there?" I asked him.

There's no delicate way to prepare you for his answer. "That's the crapper," he said, somewhat proudly, a non-gentile but completely appropriate word to encapsulate it. Yes, it was. We made some frantic calls, and the next day two very acceptable restroom trailers arrived from Toronto. Apparently, Torontonians visited the restroom in style.

"How much did you pay for those fancy crappers?" Nick asked. "I had the blue one donated by one of my ice fishing buddies."

"Okayyyy. How about transportation? We need some sort of van to fetch equipment, lunch, and worker bees," I asked Nick.

"I'll take care of it," he said.

Later that day, a van, of sorts, arrived. It had no rearview mirror. From the shotgun seat, one could see the road through the floor in two places. The back seats were a series of milk crates that were not fastened to anything. It didn't break down, though steam appeared occasionally from under the hood. We gave it as much downtime as we could.

I hesitated to ask, "Nick, I need lifts to hang the lights, drapery, and scenic."

"I'll take care of it," was his reply.

"I was afraid you were going to say that."

To my pleasant surprise, "genie" lifts (they go straight up), snorkel lifts (more like a fireman's ladder), man lifts (single occupant—straight up), and a forklift (self explanatory) began to arrive, one by one. Less to my surprise, not one of them worked for longer than twenty minutes at a time. When the first expired, I thought, "Okay, that was a fluke." The next one: "What a coincidence." The third: "Get me a mechanic and make him comfortable; he is not going anywhere." Gus arrived and for the next two days, he could be found tinkering under one of the lifts. We always checked lifts before we attempted to start them up, lest Gus be underneath it with his toolbox and duct tape. Gus tinkered faithfully while I plied him with food and drink, so he wouldn't go missing. We didn't let Gus out of our sight until the day after the wedding for load-out.

Visually, the space presented a great deal of square footage, of course more analogous to a skating rink than a fancy wedding. An equally great deal of creative ingenuity and fabric was required to approach anything resembling pizzazz. The sheer amount of equipment and supplies adding up begged yet another truck.

I cautiously asked, "Nick, I need another truck."

"I'll take care of it."

"Uh-oh…"

Gail had scoured the wholesale markets of Toronto for fabric, rentable chandeliers and candelabras, and sent it all up north on the second, actually quite decent, truck. The utilitarian ceiling and walls of the Idylwylde ice rink soon gave way to a grand, Italian pergola. The beams of the rafters, high above, lent themselves beautifully to Gail's fabric draping and Larry's lighting improvisation.

I can't ever remember our family not knowing Pat, who owned Rosemary Florists of Sudbury. Pat rose to the Hollywood-sized occasion, dressing chandeliers, candelabras, and tables with elegant arrangements of all shapes and sizes. Pat, along with Mark's Garden's Chris by her side, also commandeered every friend and relative she could to get the job done. Pat and Chris were soon two peas in a pod and fast became friends.

Okay: venue, sound, band, florals, rentals, all done. Um, oh wait, valet! Sudburians are a pretty self-sufficient group. We aren't the valet type. One doesn't valet when hunting for moose in a giant Land Rover with oversized tires, or pulling a motorboat behind a truck. But with 300 cars arriving at the same time, we needed valet. My fellow kinsmen would be obliged to surrender the keys to their precious four-wheel drives and station wagons. Jordan, the son of my good friend Shelly Lund, pulled his buddies together, who were all sent into their closets to dig out, lend each other, or buy white polo shirts and dark pants. I sent Matt to Kmart, Kresge's, and Canadian Tire to find 20 cheap, dark umbrellas.

For two full days, I pointed, Steve's buddies lugged, Gail hung, Larry lit, Pat and Chris arranged, Carol and her gang prepped, Matt shopped, Lesley, Bert, Chelsea, and MaryJane churned out paperwork, Lauren and Sasha booked staff anywhere anyhow, Corinne held my kids on her knee, and Nick "took care" of this and that.

The party was a wonderful success. Gail's décor was sublime; Pat had outdone herself with the florals. As we say in the event world, "lighting is everything", and Larry's brilliant work brought the entire creation to wonderful life. It didn't rain. Shelly's son and his car jockey friends parked the 300 cars and scored some pretty good tips. Only one car arrived pulling a boat. Carol, Sam and Christina feverishly churned out hors d'oeuvres that had been stuffed into a dozen fridges of family and friends as much as 48 hours before. As they chopped, grilled, and prepped in the kitchen tent, they basked in rave reviews trickling back from the reception via their niece and nephew waiters and waitresses. Stuart delivered a simply divine menu, as I knew he would. Dinner was the single element I had not lost one moment of sleep worrying about. The guests, rising to the occasion, ate and drank, toasted and danced until the wee hours. Finally we realized that we needed munchies to serve what turned out to be a raucous "after party". My staff reported that they handled midnight munchies in a decidedly Sudbury fashion, ordering 25 large, assorted pizzas from Cortina's, everyone's favorite local pizza joint, also open until the wee hours. The only reason the band had to stop was that the drummer's wrist became seriously swollen. By that time, I had long crawled into bed and reunited with my daughter and son. My pillow is my second biggest satisfaction after a job well done.

Cinderella Story

The wife of the President of Academy of Motion Picture Arts and Sciences screams. This is a blood-curdling scream. A fish is flopping wildly in front of her plate. Small, very much alive and a little fresher than you want fish to be served. We all sit dumbfounded for a second or two, until one of my favorite associates, Corey Taylor—floor manager of Wolfgang Puck Catering—breezes in, picks up the fish and plops it back into the decorative fish tank above our heads.

"More wine?" Corey asks with aplomb.

Suspending a fish tank above a black-tie dining table is a daring choice, apparently not without its challenges. Thank goodness the Academy has always let me think outside the box, or the bowl.

This was to be our first year at Hollywood and Highland complex, the official new home of the Oscars®, and the Academy had asked me to incorporate the existing design of the new ballroom, which was built especially for the Academy Awards® Governors Ball.

"Do not disguise the room or redo it, Cheryl; you can enhance what is already there," were the instructions.

"Sure. No problem."

I walk into the ballroom for the first time and all I can think of is fish. There was no blue, no patterns of fish; just a lot of lush, orange organza curtains draping expansive doorways of glass.

"Hmm, fish." Orange goldfish, koi, shubunkin, comets, fan-tails, Chinese goldfish. I don't know how these kind of ideas come to me, but when they come, I just go with them. Perhaps the organza was reminiscent of those fish bowls containing brightly colored pebbles and iridescent fish? I loved goldfish bowls as a child. Remember *One Fish, Two Fish, Red Fish, Blue Fish* by Dr. Seuss? It was one of my favorite books.

I wanted the fish to float above the tables so that when guests walked throughout the room, they'd mingle among the fish. Living art. Kind of Zen, right? So that's what I did. We built tables with openings cut directly through the center. The tanks would be free standing from the floor so that if the tables were nudged, the tanks wouldn't budge and the water wouldn't slosh.

We designed the fish tanks to stand six feet above the floor, on thin, unobtrusive metal legs, which did not obstruct sight lines, and formed creative spaces. In this open area directly under the tank, we arranged beautiful Cymbidium orchids among carefully placed, polished stones. The pinspot light on the tank would shine through the water and reflect onto the flowers. The illumination on the orchids rippled as the fish swam, emulating the bottom of a lush lagoon. It was meticulously orchestrated and ultimately gorgeous.

But the fish had other ideas.

Cut to several weeks before the actual event, and my illustrious staff are preparing the Governors Ball

OPPOSITE PAGE

74th Academy Awards®
Governors Ball
Nadine Froger Photography

press conference since early morning. We are about to unveil three distinct table designs to the media and to various top executives of the Academy, including the President and his wife, the Ball Chair, and the Committee. The press, waiting outside, would enter for a few moments, photograph the tables, hold some brief interviews and then depart. Finally alone, my leads and the Academy would sit together at one of the tables and enjoy a thorough tasting of Wolfgang Puck's culinary magic. The fish (mine, not Wolfgang's) had been researched, tested and, yes, rehearsed. My background is theater; I always insist on rehearsals because I leave nothing to chance.

Tropical fish experts had instructed me that we needed a strict "no feeding the fish" policy, until the press conference and tasting was over.

Someone fed the fish.

Those fish have the tiniest and quickest little digestive systems. Twenty minutes before the press were let in, the fish had to be removed and all the water changed, let's leave it at that. Somehow, the fish were returned in time to sparkling, fresh water before my clients came in. Crisis over.

The Committee—laying eyes on the tanks over the assorted tables for the first time—oohed and aahed, as we gathered and sat. Very happy with the initial response, I was about to describe the concept and detail of the design, the linens, the accenting, the choices of china and glassware, as well as the sumptuous pre-set hors d'oeuvres that lay before us.

Cue the blood-curdling scream and that renegade koi, flopping wildly. Corey—the ever consummate maître d—plopped it calmly into the water without missing a beat.

The Committee gently asked me how the experience we have all just survived would be corrected before the actual Ball. My theater training kicked into overdrive. I managed to answer all questions intelligently and with authority (though I wanted to die). Finally after about 20 minutes of diffusing the collective under-sea angst in the room, we proceeded to enjoy Wolfgang's delectable delights, as Wolfgang himself explained each hors d'oeuvre and dinner course. As ever, at a Wolfgang tasting, we happily ate too much.

Thankfully, by the time we stood and offered our goodbyes, the subject of that koi's leap to freedom had long been dropped, until Ric Robertson, the ever cheerful Executive Administrator of the Academy, said, "I am so full, I feel like a fish out of water!"

"Thanks Ric. Good one." Mixed metaphor. Nevertheless I will never forget it!

Fast forward to the day of the Ball: the fish are on their best behavior, swimming happily. The look is magnificent. We are confident that the renegade fish had just been an "odd fish".

According to plan, the ballroom is luxuriously accented with the addition of chartreuse burnt velvet linens. The two-toned tablecloths from linen specialist, Resource One, are spectacular. The ballroom is dazzling, ready and set for 1,500 of Hollywood's best. The centerpieces are assorted combinations of exotic fish and Mark's Gardens' indelible orchids.

At this point in the evening, very close to guest arrival at the ballroom, I am in constant contact with the Academy Awards broadcast that immediately precedes the Ball at the Kodak Theatre. Best Actor is about to be announced. Only two awards remain after that. 10 minutes to go. Then 1,500 guests will make their way

OPPOSITE PAGE

Wolfgang Puck's signature gold-dusted chocolate Oscars®

From left: Ball Co-Chair Cheryl Boone Isaacs, Cheryl Cecchetto, Chef Wolfgang Puck, Ball Co-Chair Sid Ganis and Academy of Motion Picture Arts and Sciences President Frank Pierson

©A.M.P.A.S.

Oscar Statuette ©A.M.P.A.S.®

from the Kodak Theatre, to the ballroom. Just as guests arrive, we'll cue the band and our doors will open.

Incredibly, a koi jumps. Then 30 seconds later, from across the ballroom, I hear commotion among the waiters. A second koi has jumped. I was completely baffled as I tested the koi several times after that fateful day at the tasting.

I'll never know what the beef was with the fish. The tanks were individually treated with filters affording their occupants plenty of clean water, the ideal temperature, and oxygen. Propped up almost three feet above the tabletops, bathed in light and complemented by those beautiful orchids, they were really the stars of our show. This was their 15 minutes; in fact, it was their three whole hours of fame. The goldfish were very happy to soak up all the attention, as were the fan fish, elegant in their under-the-sea formal wear. But apparently the koi, feeling frisky, had bigger fish to fry. Was there an after-party they needed to get to? Who knows? Whatever their problem was, they were suddenly making a swim for it. If you think I was going to wait for a third koi to jump, you are wrong. Splash me once, shame on you; but splash me twice…

Enter my tuxedoed fish wranglers (you have to have fish wranglers when you engage 2,000 frisky fish). Only two awards left to go, 10 minutes tops, my assistant repeats my shocking directive over the two-way radio to more than a hundred headsets: "All koi must be removed from all tanks."

One award to go and the fish wranglers are working as fast as they can. I am now hiking myself up onto one chair, then another, accosting each koi that needs to be removed—in my gown and heels.

In walks Ric. "What are you doing Cheryl?" He asks.

"Oh, checking out the room," I respond.

"From up there?"

"Yes, it looks great. Wanna see?" I ask.

Ric surveys the room from ground level. My managers and several Wolfgang Puck captains, with rolled up tux shirt sleeves, also standing on chairs, are elbow-deep in water.

"The fish are jumping, aren't they?" Ric asks.

"Yes Ric, the fish are jumping. (Isn't that a song?) But just the koi," I add, cheerfully.

And in his calm, cool manner, Ric says, "Is that the good news?" And then: "Are we going to make it?"

"Sure. No problem."

Final acceptance speech, two tanks to go, but we remove the koi in time.

Sorry koi, we dressed you, rehearsed you, and lit you the best we could. You succumbed to opening night jitters, but as we say in Hollywood, "The show must go on."

The koi spent the Ball sequestered in our production office, which is right next to the kitchen, in eight oversized buckets. Wolfgang thought it was hilarious. I was slightly more frazzled but eventually calmed down. All I can say is that the party went "swimmingly".

The next day, all the fish were donated to a beautiful pond in Ladera Heights, most with a Cinderella story to tell.

The Night the Lights Went On

AND OFF

In 2002, the Academy Awards® Governors Ball was produced at the Hollywood and Highland complex for the first time. The facility had not yet proven itself on such a large scale. I was continually reassured by the in-house techies that the ballroom had the proper amount of wattage, amps, and volts needed for an event of this size.

They told me, "This is exactly how much power you can pull, Cheryl," and "This is what we are allocating to you, Cheryl." What they didn't know was that someone else from the building, not in the Oscar® loop, had allocated our power to another part of the complex. Essentially, our power was double-booked.

On the big night, about an hour into the Ball, with dinner, dancing and schmoozing in full swing and the fish behaving, the emergency house lights popped on in a million-watt burst of sunlit glory, as my lights popped off. Spotlights on the band, lush scenic, up-lighting on the walls, sconce lighting, ceiling lighting, recessed lighting, even the bubbles in the fish tank; everything ceased to function.

As I've mentioned, I had been asked by the Academy not to disguise the original room that year, just to augment what was there. The newly erected ballroom had been specifically designed for the Ball, and the powers that be rightfully wanted to show off its original design. Academy, Emmy® and Grammy® award-winning composer Alan Bergman, our Ball Chair at the time, was not fond of the undressed room.

I had hung a number of additional chandeliers and augmented the existing ones. One of the purposes of event lighting is to direct the eye towards certain focal points and away from other areas—in this case, the existing ceiling. Even the soft, romantic candlelight was overtaken by the harsh fluorescents. Emergency lighting, which is completely harsh and unforgiving, sends as much light as it can in every possible direction. Think of your first stolen kiss by the dashboard light of your boyfriend's car, when the policeman suddenly shines his flashlight through the window.

Now, a 40-piece orchestra with no audio support still sounds beautiful. There was no break in Wolfgang's sumptuous food service, thanks to all the gas-powered stoves and grills, and masterminded by the amazing Matt Bencivenga, Executive Chef. The champagne was flowing. Just at the moment of the blitz, Alan Bergman had been standing in the dead center of the ballroom, exclaiming proudly to his entourage, "See how Cheryl's team, with the clever use of lighting and scenery, is redirecting our eyes to focus on design elements?" Instantaneously, our lights flickered out and the unforgiving emergency lights flared up. Alan remarked, without missing a beat, "And that's the ceiling that Cheryl didn't want us to see." Alan considered it an opportunity to continue his explanation of the décor. "Now you can see the transformation. Any questions?" Later, Alan told me he assumed I had executed this lighting change to demonstrate the effect of decor lighting. I'm pretty sure he was joking.

I appeared to be the only one who was having a nervous breakdown, at least on the outside. We reached the building engineers via cellphone to frantically explain what had happened, begging them to rush up to the fifth floor and rescue our creation from the harsh light of day. They swore to me that the dire situation I was describing to them was impossible. I begged them, "Come up and see." After summoning all the fire inspectors, building engineers, lighting directors and technicians that I could possibly find, I stood everyone in a circle faking calm, and said, "Gents, I have a party to run. I don't know how to turn the power back on, so you do what you have to do and I'll do what I have to do." What did I do? I adopted a few choice yoga poses, in my gown, one after the other, ending up in child's pose, behind a settee. I wondered if there was a restroom that I could sneak out of. I considered taking up chanting.

In fact, the party did continue. The world did not end. The guests were happy to eat and mingle, and even dance. Once I convinced the on-site fire and security personnel that there was no fire or emergency, at least they cut the emergency lights (about seven minutes after the power failure), and for a brief time, the room no longer resembled an oversized operating theater. To everyone's delight, especially mine, we languished in the glow of only table candles, and the chandelier candles suspended from the ceiling. It was actually quite enchanting. Perhaps five or 10 romantic minutes later, power was returned, our designed and directed show lighting glowed, and I could breathe again.

I walked up to Alan bravely. "I'm so sorry. I will explain everything once I find out what happened... We had 10 meetings about the power... Alan, I feel terrible."

"Cheryl, it's perfect!" Alan told me exactly how he had described everything, laughing. What a sweetheart. I tried to laugh with him. Then I gingerly approached Robert Rehme, the Academy's President at the time, devastated and ready to face the music. Robert caught my eye. I inhaled a shallow breath. Before I could speak, he said with a big smile, "Oh, Cheryl, please. You're so dramatic. Everything is fine," and returned to his guests. I exhaled a very large breath.

For six months afterwards, the power debacle permeated my every meeting and haunted my every dream. The proverbial actor's nightmare is when she dreams about being thrust out on stage but can't remember any of her lines or even being cast in a play. Surely, the event producer's nightmare is the lights going out, and the decidedly wrong ones coming on in their place. As ever, Mikel Gordon, Associate Executive Administrator of the Academy, was my rock and positive reinforcement as I called, interrogated, calculated, and reassessed, until I finally did get to the bottom of the power struggle and miscalculation. Apparently, and completely unknown to the venues engineering leads, a whole other section of the facility had also tapped into our specific power allocation, thus overloading our allotment. Fourteen years later, I still fight the urge to plug our lighting in myself.

Curtain Call

INXS IN EXCESS

In 2003, the G'DAY LA (now G'DAY USA) events were conceived to strengthen the relationship between Australia and the U.S. in business, innovation, and culture. Wally Mariani, Qantas Senior Executive Vice President to the Americas required an event producer, and was proffered a strong recommendation of Sequoia Productions by the President of the Los Angeles Sports and Entertainment Commission. The effervescent Wally walked me into a G'DAY LA Committee meeting and announced, "Sequoia Productions is the company we need to spearhead our Los Angeles events, hands down." Okay... no pressure.

In 2006, our third G'DAY USA Black Tie celebration was booked at the legendary Hollywood Palladium, where icons such as Tommy Dorsey, Frank Sinatra, and Glenn Miller had once headlined. None other than INXS agreed to perform, as they were also scheduled to receive an award of recognition that night. It was quite the coup to book them for an intimate gathering of only 600 diners, as they typically performed in stadiums to many thousands of screaming fans. Score! Perhaps the fact that it was an occasion celebrating Australia and Australians, also populated with Australian guests, that clinched the deal. As a Canadian, I was super excited that INXS had only just signed on the dynamic Canadian, J.D. Fortune, as their new lead singer. INXS had agreed to play three of their long list of hits: *Never Tear Us Apart, Need You Tonight*, and *Afterglow*. Their road manager assured the Honorable John Olsen, Australian Consul General in Los Angeles at the time, that their 15-minute set, beginning at 8:30 p.m. was firm, as we were on a strict timetable. In a word, John was an important, well-known dignitary, as former Premier of South Australia, rightfully commanding respect and all due consideration.

The red carpet arrivals ran long, as media outlets each clamored to claim their own individual interviews and photos with Eric Bana, Hugh Jackman, Olivia Newton-John, Naomi Watts and John Travolta. We were already behind schedule, with the program not yet started. Once our show was underway, the clock continued to tick as presenters and honorees delivered slightly more effusive and thankful (read: long) speeches than we had anticipated. Unlike at the Oscars®, there was no orchestra poised to play soft, suggestive exit music after 45 seconds. Following the opening program that included the delightful Qantas Girls Choir and an awards presentations to Olivia and Hugh, the moment everyone had been waiting for finally arrived. INXS took to the stage.

Barbra Held, my client, is a woman of extraordinary integrity, intelligence and stamina. In other words, she is my kind of girl. Barb is intimately involved in all aspects of the production and she always joins me at the Front of House, during a show. By the time INXS began their performance, the overall show was 35 minutes behind schedule. Barb and I were already in deep discussion about the time element and how we might trim the

program. The reality of any event production is once the show begins it must be allowed to live, to breathe in a life of its own. Barb and I did just that.

Did I mention that INXS were no less than sensational? And the guests were having the time of their lives. All good. Fantastic and crowd-pleasing as they already are, they were playing to their own, adoring compatriots. Suddenly half the crowd burst forth from their elegant dinner tables and rushed to the stage, in typical ready-to-party Australian form. The area down in front, including the first row of VIP tables, transformed into a mostly over-30s mosh pit. J.D. rocked it, and grown up guests-turned-teenagers rocked right along with him. From the children of dignitaries to the over-65 set, all danced their hearts out and sang along, not that you could hear next to the sub-woofer speakers. One, two, three hits flew by, as an increasing number of Aussies ran up to join the fray.

ABOVE
11th Annual G'DAY USA
Black Tie Gala
Johnny Cho
Photo courtesy of ELS

Of course, you know what rock stars do when they are killing it? After the frenzied finish of the third song, J.D. and the gang bowed and waved, feigning all the goodbyes and thank yous that one expects of a beloved rock band allegedly about to leave the stage, then dove into a triumphant encore. The crowd jumped and cheered in excitement. Wait! What about our 15-minute deal? There were still a few speeches ahead, as well as a grand finale with the choir returning, singing *I Still Call Australia Home* and featuring an unannounced appearance by Hugh Jackman.

Guests trickling, then pouring out of a ballroom when dignitaries are still speaking is a sure sign that the party has gone on too long. There are times when a party assumes a life of its own, usually in a good way, and there's really nothing you can do; nothing wrong with being held hostage by one's own success, right?

Wrong. Surrendering, I indulged in a little spontaneous dancing of my own over to the side of the room, along with a few enchanted waiters who weren't actually supposed to be dancing. By rights, neither was I. I noticed the Honorable John Olsen veritably jogging in my direction. The expression on his face as he swiftly descended upon me confirmed that he was definitely not in the mood for dancing. John landed at a spot a good 15 feet from me, actually rather close to two guest tables, where a few stragglers were enjoying the band from their seats. From there he launched, at the top of his lungs, a barrage of scheduling discontent in my direction. Perhaps John instinctively felt that he needed plenty of buffer between us, such was his anger at that moment for such a blatant assault on his timetable.

It was difficult to hear him, but I did hear the phrase, "and THIS IS… NOT… ON!" I had not heard that definitely Aussie expression before, but the look on John's face confirmed that he could not abide the show running any later than it had already.

Flustered, I disappeared backstage, figuring I could put whatever "it" was back "on". But of course, I could not. What I didn't know was that John had followed me. Considering the volume around us and now right next to the band, he had to tap my shoulder to get my attention, then shout again. This time I don't know what he said, I probably heard it, but I don't remember it. What registered was that he was raising his voice to me. A tenet of mine is that yelling throws cold water on the spirit of a project and hurts morale. It's not the right vibe, and not how I ride. Not that I haven't raised my voice in my life, especially to my kids, but I always regret it.

I answered, inches from his ear so I could be heard, yet with decorum, "John, I understand," I said, "but I don't know what I can do. I can't walk up there and unplug J.D.'s guitar."

Thankfully, we didn't experience any trickling or pouring out once INXS left the stage. Guests raved over Curtis' desserts as they nursed their coffee and many didn't show signs of leaving any time soon.

Water long under the bridge, John and I now love to tell our story, sometimes standing right next to each other, finishing each other's sentences. All said and done, John and I share the same goal—to support the event's theme and to ensure that every guest enjoys a rip-roaring, Aussie good time. The party was wonderfully successful on both counts. As kindred spirits in that regard, it goes without saying that John and I share a fondness for each other as well.

But wait, the night wasn't over yet…

Oh, But I Insist

THE SHOW MUST GO ON

The INXS set ended with a deafening flourish; a triumph. I headed to the technical booth at the back of the ballroom, wondering if my ears would be able to hear the rest of the show's cues in my headset. On the way, I pulled a waiter captain aside and nodded discreetly at John's table (fine dining rule number 27-D: never, ever point).

"Drown table #402 in champagne," I instructed. "Kill them with kindness. Also, ask them how much they enjoyed INXS!"

I resumed my position next to the technical director to close out the show. As I mentioned, we were now approaching the grand finale, with the Qantas Girls Choir singing *I Still Call Australia Home*, and featuring Hugh Jackman as a surprise soloist. Just as I sat, a small man walked up to me briskly, his eyes firmly fixed on mine. Now what? I then recognized him as Hugh Jackman's manager, though most of my dealings with him had been via email. He reminded me of Tom Cruise's zany character in *Tropic Thunder*, though unlike Tom, he didn't appear to be in the mood for dancing. There was no greeting.

"Hugh won't be singing in the finale. It's not in his key," he announced and turned to leave. For just a moment I was dumbfounded, but that's a very temporary state for me.

After what was perhaps only a second, I replied, "What? I don't understand. It's all rehearsed!"

He repeated himself, this time very tersely: "Hugh won't be singing." He turned, a second time, to walk away. Before I could think of a retort or suggest a solution, he disappeared into the crowd.

My mind raced. The finale was only 10 minutes away, with Hugh's blocking, lighting, microphone and harmony all rehearsed with the choir and technicians, written into the printed cues, and burned into the minds of every cameraman and stagehand. The day before, as soon as the Jackman camp had committed to his surprise performance, I had immediately notified all parties, especially the choir's choreographer, in order to adjust for this huge opportunity. Hugh had not rehearsed, but the Qantas Choir completely re-choreographed around a Hugh Jackman stand-in the day before. Halfway through the final reprise, the choir had been directed to majestically part like the Red Sea for Hugh "Moses" Jackman's entrance, front and center, then settle themselves around him in enraptured adoration, singing supporting harmonies. Suddenly, the choir was destined to adulate around a gaping, empty space.

Hugh was a major star in Hollywood at the time, having starred in *The Boy from Oz* on Broadway, and the *X-Men* films. At rehearsal, the promise of singing with Aussie icon Hugh Jackman and possibly snagging a group picture had the Qantas Choir all a-flutter. I rushed backstage, down the hall, and burst through the door into their green room. Forty girls looked up with their shining, cherubic faces, their pending performance with

Mr. Jackman so close at hand. As popular and fresh as Hugh already was in the U.S., in Australia, he was huge.

I think my particular fondness of Australian youngsters derives from my only contact with them, and that's via the Qantas Choir. I've produced the G'DAY USA Gala going on twelve years. They are the most polite, scrubbed and polished, every-hair-in-place, grateful, delightful group of kids you'd ever want to meet. Every time they return, I want to adopt every one of them. As they sat there in palpable anticipation, I realized I simply couldn't let them down, not after a 7,500-mile flight. My heart melted. I delivered the broadest, incredibly convincing fake smile I could muster.

"Have a great show, girls!" is all that escaped my mouth.

"Thank you very much, Cheryl!" they all chirped back in chorus. I closed the door as briskly as I had opened it.

I was in big trouble. My mind raced again. Eureka! I suddenly realized the solution, which is so often the solution in emergency situations. Cut out the middleman. I squared my shoulders, deciding that I would find and convince Hugh myself, somehow. I could hear my mother's voice ringing in my ears, "Be bold Cheryl. Make a choice, commit, and go for it." I thought to myself, "This one's for you, Mum." As a producer, and

ABOVE

11th Annual G'DAY USA
Black Tie Gala performance
by Qantas Girls Choir with
William Barton

Jerick Dizon

especially as a mother, I pick my battles. Today, I picked this one. I'll do it for the girls. I wasn't the client, mind you. I was the producer; the producer, working on the client's behalf. My strategy to approach Hugh directly could well go south, and I'd be in deep doo-doo. I looked at my watch. He really should have been set backstage already. I jogged back down the hall to the ballroom, pressing my headset to my head with one hand and clutching the radio with the other, lest the entire gizmo bounce right off of me. I paused only to switch my radio from the Show Channel #7 to Ballroom Channel #1, where the floor staff resided, "Find Hugh Jackman!" I announced. I resumed jogging.

"Hugh is walking to the back of the room," was the reply. Re-entering the ballroom I rushed across as quickly as I could, without actually running (rule number 16-D: never run past guests, no matter the issue at hand). I assumed my black-tie, ballroom-appropriate stride, resembling the low impact, fast-walk that your neighbors perform past your living room window every morning, only in my case, without the mini barbells. My thirteenth hour on the job, and with rehearsal dragging past 11 p.m. the night before, I may as well have been carrying mini barbells, too. We were so close to the finish line, and I was determined to cross it with Hugh Jackman. I managed not to knock anyone over nor spill anyone's glass of champagne (yes, two more golden rules).

Easy to spot, there he was, 6' 2" as ever, surrounded by mostly female admirers—all with cameras, all aggressively jockeying for a position to take selfies with him, photo after cherished photo. I didn't have time for decorum; I was about to reach him via a generous application of elbows. Suddenly, it was Hugh himself who masterfully, gracefully broke away from the pack, making a beeline to the men's room. I followed him. I was stalking Hugh Jackman; that was clear. I somehow retained the good sense to not actually follow him in. I waited at the door, hopefully looking nonchalant. Hugh popped out again, sure to be inundated by another gaggle of fans on the way back to his table. I pounced.

With a mixture of delight and authority, I reintroduced my effusive, fake smile under duress: "Hugh! There you are." I smiled again. "Are you having a good time? We need you on stage right away for the finale!" Hugh looked only slightly startled and may have tried to speak, but I felt strongly that I mustn't let him get a word in. My inner actress kicked in: "Phew! I'm glad I found you. This is going to be wonderful, the girls are so looking forward to it." I rambled away, as I gently coaxed him to walk in the direction of the stage. I spoke louder than anyone in our earshot. We eventually assumed quite a pace, with me slightly in the lead, blocking and evading well-wishers. Hugh smiled and kept up, ever charming. Sensing the urgency, he deferred a few well-wishers himself.

"I'm needed on stage," he said a few times with a broad smile. Perhaps he had only mentioned to his manager in passing, "Hmm, I'm a little concerned about the key. What do you think?" or something like that, and his manager had taken it from there. Even the most modest and appreciative of movie stars are accustomed to their people falling over themselves to provide for their every whim and want; God bless his manager. Everyone does their level best for their client. This was me doing my best for mine and for the girls.

We arrived at stage right simultaneously with half the Qantas Choir, so I knew the other half of the choir was positioning stage left. Perfect. On cue, 20 girls cooed and giggled around him, some introducing themselves as I handed him a hand-held microphone. Hugh was lovely with them. I was pretty charmed myself. I'm sure that if Hugh had still harbored any doubts about the key, the girls cinched the deal. The choir's chaperones swiftly relieved several of them of their cameras. I introduced him to a stagehand, who positioned him at the off-stage staircase. Okay!

I trekked back to the booth as the finale announced itself with a flourish. I avoided Hugh's table with a wide arc because that was where his manager would be sitting. Once again I caught the captain's eye who trotted over.

"Send a few tall waiters over to table #22 to bus empty plates and basically fuss. Pour some water, shake out some napkins, and try to obscure the stage a bit—no, a lot!"

The captain's face betrayed his confusion, but he just answered, "No problem." That's my kind of captain.

The music track announced the beginning of the end; the first strains of Australia's officially, unofficial anthem and favorite song. The girls entered in perfect choreography with huge smiles, singing their hearts out. The music ascended with bravado, supposedly beyond Hugh Jackman's favorite key. Hugh sailed onto the stage with a flourish. Two cameras followed Hugh and the choir, their images projected brightly across 50-foot screens on each side of the stage. The audience applauded warmly. Hugh sang beautifully and with authority. The last word of the last line, "I still call Australia hooooome," was perhaps a little out of Hugh's reach. Nobody would have guessed. Hugh adjusted expertly to the harmonic note below, in that commanding singing voice that had snagged him the Tony in 2004. The upper, tonic note rang out via six sopranos, who were supposed to sing it anyway. The audience stood and cheered. Hugh and the girls beamed and bowed. Photos were snapped. The curtain closed. The show ended a full 45 minutes late, every minute worth it; it was smashing success.

My last remaining task for the evening was to extend a few thank yous for a job well done, while evading Hugh Jackman's manager, as well as realizing that the Honourable John and I might need a little space. I couldn't return to the booth, which both John and the manager knew was my regular perch. I buzzed around to thank a few of the major clients, basically bobbing and weaving stealthily until I walked to my car. "Move like a butterfly, run like the wind." That's not exactly what Muhammad Ali said, but it worked for me.

"You're going to get into a little trouble every day," my dad would say. When you're right, Dad, you're right. Sorry I didn't manage to get that out of the way before noon.

True to their Down-Under reputations, the Australians and their admirers finally did depart, though the majority of them merely shifted over to the after-party to revel into the night. Lingering guests, oblivious to the fact that I'd worked a 14-hour day, indicate the ultimate "hats off" to a terrific party. I love Australians!

Green M&Ms

His name goes to my grave, considering that he almost put me there himself, but here's my brief one-night-stand with so-and-so.

Relentlessly publicized, press-released, red-carpeted and paparazzi'd, the G'DAY USA Gala guarantees major publicity for invited and awarded international celebrities from Down Under, and limelight for their native land.

I kid you not, we negotiated about 100 phone calls and emails with this particular star's four representatives, three assistants, two drivers, and a housekeeper (well, it felt like it), who demanded everything except, ironically, no green M&Ms. You've possibly heard the story about how some famous movie star once included, in his substantial rider, a request for M&Ms in his trailer, but with the green ones taken out. This caveat was not due to an aversion to certain M&Ms. It was, in fact, a secret ploy to ensure that any unsuspecting producer had actually read all the fine print of the rider. Now a famous fable in the entertainment industry, I'm sure many a star's road manager has repeated this clandestine test in many a rider. I prefer the brown M&Ms myself, but still…

This particular star's demands included (and I can't even remember it all):

Call #37: Star requires three exclusive, stocked green rooms (star ultimately never sets foot in any of them).

Call #49: Star is considering attending, but will not rehearse. I can't even imagine this, but star has already become my personal nightmare ever since call #37.

Call #54: Star requires dedicated security team.

Call #62: Green rooms require a brand of tea that we must have shipped from Canberra. The cost probably works out to about $24 a bag. I would rather have rooted out each green M&M myself.

Call #68: Star commits (well, sort of).

Call #79: (The big day) "Oh my Lord, where is he?" Limo has been waiting for the star at the hotel for an hour and a half, and call time has come and gone. Okay, heart palpitations.

Live show begins: Star is not seated at his table. Frantic cuts of camera cues on star's table to save his reputation as "somebody who cares".

Radio call: "Star has arrived", at the loading dock next to the dumpsters. I abandon my post as show director and rush down the kitchen hallways, past rows of waiting desserts and coffee.

Star carefully never looks at me or refers to me by name, as he walks with his acting coach and sister, never looking up at an adoring Red Sea of surprised waiters, parting to let him pass. Hmm. I was a waiter once. I smiled at the waiters, hoping to fill the void.

Star announces, "I'll receive the award from backstage!" I'm not often speechless. Amazingly, I think of something. I politely inform star, "The award is presented Academy Award® style, with you then taking the stage from your table to receive it, expressing your humble appreciation." I resist the temptation to define the word humble. Truthfully, I don't actually say the world humble. Pick your battles, right? "Oh, Academy Award style?" "Yes," I say. Star agrees. I rest my case about the humble part.

ABOVE

8th Annual G'DAY USA

Black Tie Gala fashion show

presented by Myer

Line 8 Photography

Photo courtesy of ELS

Star arrives at waiters' entrance to the ballroom and says to me, still never looking, "You can go now." Oh. Thank you.

Star graciously accepts his award. Star is handsome, charming, self-effacing. Star clearly deserves this award; he is a really good actor. He then modestly changes the subject to talk about his non-profit organization. That obliges me to warm to him a little. Fine. I feel a little guilty now about writing the rest of this, but I'll survive.

Star departs the stage and insists on returning to his limo once again, camera shots of his table are hastily deleted once more from the show rundown.

At this point, star's security team is enjoying exclusive use of his green rooms, and what had better be some pretty darned good Australian tea.

Seated in the limo, star says, "Would you please tell my manager and my brother that I'm ready to leave?" Now he's talked to me twice.

I dutifully hunch my way over to the manager's table, dead center and up-front, skulking below the spotlight. I whisper into brother's ear. He replies, "It would be rude to leave before the last award is presented. I'm not going anywhere." I like him immediately. Maybe Australian apples fall far from the eucalyptus tree.

I return to the loading dock with the unwelcome news. Star returns begrudgingly to the table through the kitchen. At the kitchen door, I am told that "I may go" (again). I appreciate that. I wonder what I will do with my time.

A few moments later, one of my cameramen catches a perfect shot of star smiling and applauding from his table. The image is displayed on two huge screens to the entire ballroom, and immediately instagrammed, tweeted and tooted all over the world. Success.

Star needs to be escorted back to the limo, through the kitchen, as his manager can't remember the way. I'd prefer to go meet the security guards and sample this epic tea, but…

I escort them all back to the waiting limo and close the door. He may go.

If you only knew. Well, now you do.

* * *

I've witnessed, first hand, the gratitude and generosity of so many celebrities and high-profile executives in the entertainment world. Many have assumed the roles of spokespersons for philanthropic organizations or created their own charities. Hats off to them all. It is my honor to do my part, setting the stage for their celebrations.

The Dog Squad

UNDER THE TABLE

It was 2006 and as always, our mandate for the Academy Awards® Governors Ball was to execute a 180 degree departure from past Sequoia creations. That's the challenge and thrill of a valued repeat client. Many months before, I had been staring at that crystal teardrop chandelier at the Fairmont Hotel, Vancouver Airport. The chandelier posed a question, "Cheryl, how about a massive teardrop chandelier at the Governors Ball?" it suggested.

"What would that look like?" I asked back.

"Well, perhaps not just a chandelier, but a ceiling treatment that encompasses the length and breadth of the ballroom." A tall order. Nevertheless, at the Governors Ball, every seat is a VIP seat, so the décor around the periphery must never read as an afterthought.

Hmm, I thought. Okay. What if the crystals glowed in a kaleidoscope of color, morphing every 15 minutes or so from blue to mauve to red; a modern twist on a classic theme?

As soon as the chandelier had said its piece, the practical side of my brain kicked in. How would we accomplish this? Who would design the technical specifications? What materials would be best? Is a ceiling-wide chandelier even possible, and within the budget? Where do we begin?

Returning to L.A., I mentioned the chandelier idea to my colleague, Nelson Sosa, an artisan with whom I've had the pleasure of realizing some very diverse and unique décor projects over many years, and Yummi Park, Sequoia Productions' stellar project manager.

I explained, "The ceiling should resemble a series of multi-layered, horizontal "haircuts" for lack of a better analogy, constructed from one simple material, and repeated symmetrically from 10,000 points."

"Okay, Cheryl," Nelson said, and then he disappeared for two days.

Nelson will always get back to you, though sometimes two days after you call. On-site, Nelson can't hold onto a two-way radio for more than five minutes. "Nelson, come in please. Hello Nelson? Where are you Nelson?" Oh, but Nelson, how you make up for it with sheer creative genius. Nelson doesn't render, nor provide engineered drawings. Instead he disappears into the resource jungle known as downtown Los Angeles, where ideas call out to any creative person from every fabric store, import outlet, and swap meet (flea market). Two days later, Nelson returned to my office presenting a carefully sanded and smoothed opaque tube, a number of lighting gels (clear, colored sheets that add color to light), and a simple flashlight. He shined the flashlight through the red gel into the tube and voilà, the sanded surface of the tube picked up the light and the entire tube glowed in an incandescent red. He repeated the demonstration with a blue gel, then green, then mauve. It was beautiful and simple, though Nelson and I knew that the plan

OPPOSITE PAGE

78th Academy Awards®
Governors Ball
Nadine Froger Photography
Oscar Statuette ©A.M.P.A.S.®

Raining on My Parade

In 2006, at the 117th Tournament of Roses Parade, "It's Magical", Justice Sandra Day O'Connor served as Grand Marshal. In the Parade's 125-year history, officials had only considered canceling due to weather on one other occasion. In 2006, they considered canceling again; it hadn't rained on the Pasadena's internationally famous celebration since 1955.

The two-minute opening performance begins at precisely 8 a.m. leading the way for the parade that starts at 8:02 a.m. There is no holding the curtain as the event is televised internationally to an audience of countless millions. Hired to produce this performance, my company and I commenced tackling the design and entertainment of two action-packed, impeccably timed minutes, as well as the massive behind-the-scenes logistics involved.

The opening performance is presented and broadcast live, in the middle of Orange Grove Boulevard, perpendicular to Colorado Boulevard, which is the beginning of the parade route. We installed production trailers, staff trailers, performers' green room tents, generators, restrooms and dumpsters; we shared the area with show production, a fire truck, police cars, and ambulances, all a rosebud's throw from the performance. This installation commenced two days prior and was dubbed "The Compound".

Prior to positioning our prefab stage in place for final rehearsal, dozens of floats, horse brigades and marching bands from around the country and around the world would drive through that exact spot in the wee hours of the morning. They would traverse literally miles down Orange Grove Boulevard to stage, in order, and wait. Once they had passed us, we would assemble our stage, built on two flatbeds, for dress rehearsal. During our performance, our stage would temporarily block their access to the parade route. Completely. We were required to drive our set out of the way at 8:02 a.m. sharp, as soon as our performance ended, so that the parade could commence. The length of one television commercial, 60 seconds, was all the time we were allowed to vacate the premises before the parade began.

We had secured LeAnn Rimes as headliner and designed an ambitious set, including multiple aerial performers spinning from a 50-foot truss structure. On cue, LeAnn would magically pop up onto the multi-tiered stage atop an ascending platform, as an additional thirty costumed performers danced around her.

One week out, long-term weather forecasts already predicted the possibility of trouble brewing. Los Angeles weather in the summer months is so reliable that very elaborate events are often designed for the outdoors; so unlikely is the chance of rain. In January, not so much. As the days marched on, the inevitability of rain, and a lot of it, was increasingly clear.

Rain on a parade is such an unmitigated nightmare, it's actually cliché. Emergency meetings were called.

Additional tenting was installed, wooden pathways were laid across grassy areas, and electrical cables were moved to higher ground. I sent a runner to Kmart to purchase thirty rain ponchos and twenty umbrellas. Our call time the morning of the parade was 4 a.m. The rain came and went, then came and went, often pausing for fifteen minutes or so, just to raise false hopes and then rain again. We quickly designed an attractive canopy over LeAnn's perch on stage, lest her two-minute number more resemble running through a sprinkler. Dancers and aerialists were frantically re-choreographed under artificial lighting, altering certain moves that would otherwise be too dangerous on wet surfaces. As we improvised and adjusted, Hair and Makeup accosted me at least every hour, attempting time and time again to dry my hair and reapply my make up for interviews. I told them, "Don't worry! I surrendered long ago. When it rains, it pours!"

All that early morning, Rose Parade officials deliberated. The rain was a nuisance, with the wind gusting up to 45 miles per hour. The greatest risk was the lightning, considering the tall metal grandstands holding thousands of people.

Mother Nature did not tease us during rehearsal, nor through the performance. She hammered down on us with a vengeance. It rained; it poured. But the show went on. LeAnn Rimes was a trooper. She had planned to wear these very cute short shorts. Not waiting for her to ask, I offered that she wear something a little warmer, but no, that was what she was going to wear. Just before the 6 a.m. dress rehearsal in the rain, LeAnn asked very politely, "Cheryl, do you mind terribly if I don't sing at the rehearsal in full voice? It's just a little early."

"LeAnn," I said, "you are so sweet. You do what you have to do, just don't float away on me."

After two days of preparation, improvisation, and scrambling, the actual performance at 8 a.m. just flew by, as two minutes are bound to do, and beautifully so. One dancer stumbled on the wet pavement, but recovered beautifully. Nobody fell from the sky. There was appropriately 'thunderous' applause.

At the final note of LeAnn's song, VP Gary's only job was to direct 30 people with 30 push brooms to immediately sweep away the 72 pounds of biodegradable confetti streamers, shot from 36, double confetti cannons. The parade included several equestrian groups amongst all those floats. Horses are skittish around bits of moving paper. You'd think that confetti would absorb rain, get soggy and stay in one place. No such luck. First up was a 30-piece band marching alongside 30 horses. They were grand and fabulous, and we didn't need a spooked stallion ejecting a sousaphone player into the stands, sousaphone included. Gary had rehearsed his crew several times, even incorporating prop confetti. We had thought of everything— we thought. There they were, thirty sweepers lined in military precision, dressed all in black, shoulder-to-shoulder and broom-to-broom, ready to defend against the confetti onslaught. For once, Mother Nature smiled upon us. A huge gust of wind, in tornado fashion, actually swept up the confetti in a giant swoosh and plopped it in a five-foot diameter pile in the middle of the street. I would not have believed it. Suddenly we didn't need thirty sweepers, we needed two shovels. Nevertheless, the confetti was spirited away just as the majestic horses marched past, and the parade began.

Preoccupied as I was, I couldn't help fretting about my two wet children Mia and Milan—eight and six years old at the time—sitting in the stands since 6:30 a.m. with my assistant, Argelia, probably soaked to the bone. Checking in with them at 9 a.m. they had already returned to the car, wet and cold. I heard Mia fretting in the

background, as Argelia explained that one of her shoes was floating down Orange Grove Boulevard on its way to the Pacific.

"Forget the shoe," I said. "Just get the kids home and into a hot shower. I'm right behind you."

As magical as a rainforest, a tropical cruise, and the fountains at the Bellagio Hotel all rolled into one, the 117th Rose Parade was also just as wet; five inches of rain in 24 hours.

The 2006 Rose Parade, entitled "It's Magical" proved that magic is what you make it.

Producing the relentlessly wet but ultimately exhilarating Tournament of Roses Parade opening had been a marvelous experience for my whole team.

I thought to myself, "Terrific, we've produced the Rose Parade. Big success. I'm grateful. What wonderful clients. (Still my friends, we occasionally have tea together.) Let's definitely cross Rose Parade off our list… in ink."

A year and a half later, I receive a call from the Tournament of Roses, requesting we present a proposal to produce the 2009 parade opening. I was about to very graciously decline, in favor of my pillow, when I was informed that this year's parade was to be entitled Hats Off to Entertainment.

Oh-oh, the theater arts major somewhere deep inside of me asked, did they have to name it that? How can I not produce it?

Cloris Leachman, Emmy® and Oscar®-winning actress, was confirmed as Grand Marshal. Cloris, who has attended a number of our events, is an extroverted, absolutely off-the-wall riot. The woman is relentlessly hilarious, does and says what she wants, and what she usually wants is that everybody around her be in stitches, whatever the situation.

The 95th Rose Bowl college football game has long been associated with the Tournament of Roses Parade, and is now the highest attended American college football game of the year. This year's game featured the University of Southern California Trojan's vying for a third win. The excitement was palpable.

We built a huge, black top hat as our multi-leveled stage. Once again, we constructed it atop a flatbed truck, as we were again required to vacate the street immediately after our show. Multiple Grammy® winner Gregg Field thrilled us by accepting the gig. We hired forty dynamite dancers and put them through their paces. Gregg put together a band of studio veterans recording the back-up track for none other than Billboard winner, saxophonist Dave Koz.

As 8 a.m. approached, our massive top hat set was driven into place and locked down. DJ Cory pumped up the audience. The show opened, Dave rocked it and the show was a hit, judging by the roar of a gratefully dry, sun-drenched crowd. I realized that the experience was once again worth enduring 48 hours of sleep deprivation, especially including the added perk of dry feet. No monsoons. No gale force winds. Nothing went wrong. Almost. I called Gary, our VP who had on this occasion watched the show comfortably on his big cushy couch in PJs.

"Gary, how was it?" I asked.

"Cheryl, it was fantastic!" Then, the pause, "But who were the voices?"

"What voices?" I had no idea what he was talking about.

"Voices saying, 'Pass the popcorn. Cool float, right? Can I have another donut?'" Gary said plainly. "Voices."

"I don't understand."

"Cheryl," he said, "we were hearing voices."

I jogged over to the broadcast trailer.

"Guys, can I see the playback?" I asked. The broadcast technicians, now fully involved in the parade itself, were watching perhaps a dozen television monitors, each monitor dedicated to a camera on the parade route. They huddled in concentration, deciding in the moment which camera feed to choose to send to the millions of viewers. It's called a live edit, and requires 100 percent attention.

"Cheryl, not until the parade's over," I was told in a tone of, 'Seriously?'

As the parade came to a close, I trotted back to the trailer. They played the tape. We watched and listened. The show was terrific. I was about to ask for a copy, when I did hear someone faintly say, "Pass the popcorn," right along with Dave Koz's rocking riffs. It was soft enough to not distract too much, but definitely there. A warm-up artist's responsibility is to raise the temperature in the audience to one of excitement and anticipation. DJ Cory did the trick, supported by audience mics, which enabled the audience to hear their own, amplified cheering and singing. Well, once the show begins, one obviously wants to hear Dave Koz, not the audience. Someone didn't turn off the audience mics and the whole world may have heard a few excited fans sharing a little junk food breakfast and otherwise enjoying the show. At least the whole world knew they were having a good time.

Enemy Anemones

THE UNDERSEA WORLD OF ANDY WARHOL

I have been so honored and fortunate to produce the Primetime Emmys® Governors Ball for 17 years. The reason is Geriann McIntosh. In March of 2008, heaven shone upon me when Geriann arrived at the Shrine Auditorium for a private tour of the Academy Awards® Governors Ball, which was taking shape at the time. We hit it off immediately. We share the same sensibilities, priorities, work ethic and taste! Geriann has either Chaired, Co-Chaired, or been on the Ball Committee for practically all of 17 years. Early on, we became, and have remained, valued business associates and fast friends.

The 2011 Television Academy's Governors Ball Chair, Joe Stewart, is one of those people you are so happy to have in your world. Joe simply loves life. With every vibrant word, every sweep of his arms in grand, conductor-like fashion, Joe instinctively rouses the team in common purpose, reminding everyone how much fun they are having, and rendering the world a little smaller and a lot friendlier. Joe's larger-than-life personality bodes well for what is described as "the largest annual formal sit-down dinner in the country". You have to ask yourself, can anybody actually be this happy? He sets the best example I've ever seen.

"How are youuuuu?" initiates his every greeting, whether he's speaking to the cleaning crew or an Academy executive.

"Everyone! Everyone! Let's throw a fabulous black and white ball!" Joe trumpeted at our first Primetime Emmys Governors Ball committee meeting in February. Joe's ideas burst forth with the fervor and enthusiasm of 20 cheerleaders on the field. My mind spun with the possibilities.

"A classic, black and white theme," Joe continued.

"Driven by a bold, theatrical twist!" I countered.

"Yes. Yes!" Joe exclaimed.

"Andy Warhol!" I added, trying to keep up with Joe's energy and lust for life.

"Oh yes!" answered Joe.

"Rather than serene Art Deco, we could go with a startling, psychedelic '60s design," I continued.

"But no Campbell's soup cans!" Joe laughed.

"It's a deal," I replied. Kindred spirits are few and far between. I can count mine on one hand. When I meet one, I don't let go.

As the theme for the Black and White Ball evolved, I experimented with countless possibilities of how a theme we ultimately coined "Mod Illusions", might surprise, transform, and especially "move" over the course of the evening. I envisioned an emerging fantasy, delivered to a Hollywood crowd who may well believe they have already seen everything. We placed "living art" performers on platforms throughout the room. Just

when one might assume that they were statues, they would suddenly morph to another pose. We also staged numerous, seemingly impromptu "atmosphere" performances, some entering and exiting unexpectedly from various points to musical flourishes. Others were suspended from the ceiling, while still others weaved through the guests in stylized mime fashion, all decked in surreal court jester and circus-esque costumes. Multiple surprise sensations, deceptions, and figments of the imagination were the goal.

From the wildlife documentaries I love to watch, I had recalled how the black and white patterns on zebras are designed by Mother Nature to actually confuse predators because it's difficult for a leopard to focus on his prey when he can't distinguish one zebra from another. The brilliant Kevin Lee and his company, LA Premier, with this in mind, fashioned exotic flower arrangements in geometrically varied vase "structures", reflecting the décor of the surrounding room in a bold black and white mosaic.

As a youngster, I was enthralled by the television series *The Undersea World of Jacques Cousteau*. I admired Cousteau's deep appreciation of the diverse beauty of the sea and his courage to explore that uncharted world. In one episode, Cousteau highlighted the enigmatic, alien-like sea anemone, with a fascination that

ABOVE
63rd Primetime Emmys®
Governors Ball Grey Goose
Ice Bar
Nadine Froger Photography
©ATAS/NATAS

I fully shared. These transparent, saucer-like creatures undulated hypnotically through the water, their long tentacles dangling gracefully. I imagined how the ethereal, otherworldliness of the sea anemone might lend itself to the world we were creating for the Ball.

I spoke to Irma Hardjakusumah, technical designer extraordinaire, asking her, "Irma, sea anemones… they'd ripple and swell over the Ball, elongating, contracting, spinning. What do you think?"

"Give me a few days, Cheryl", was the reply.

Irma and I are birds of a feather; my right-brain tickles her left-brain. Irma came back to me with very specific technical renderings of giant, fully functional, motorized anemone chandeliers, fashioned with strings of beads, connected to winches and cables in the ceiling. Irma's model was technically brilliant and construction of anemone chandeliers was approved.

For the past several years, the Primetime Emmys Governors Ball has featured a raised, 60-foot-wide circular dance floor. This dance floor surrounds a raised revolving stage, which has an additional 10-foot platform at

its center—ultimately 15 feet above the main floor constructed by the incredible, scenic fabricators, Bill Ferrel company. This centered stage ensured that every guest experienced his or her seat as part of the VIP section. Sheri Ebner, the Television Academy's Director of the Emmy Awards, sat each table with absolute precision, all 4,000 guests. Wow, Sheri! As the Ball approached, we became increasingly excited by the dynamic fantasy that we had extrapolated from a simple, tried and true, black and white palette.

The first of two Emmy nights is the Emmys Creative Arts Ball, honoring many technical awards among other categories. After the Emmys Creative Arts Ball, and until the following weekend, West Hall A at the Los Angeles Convention Center awaits in darkness and is then reset with fresh flowers and linen for the Emmys Governors Ball. The moment the doors opened on our first night, costumed performers held back sequined drapes at the guests' point of entry, much like living brooches pinned to a flowing ballgown. The performers also mounted pedestals to assume their statue poses. Upon her arrival, the incorrigible Emmy and Academy Award winner Cloris Leachman found herself mesmerized by these performers. Suddenly realizing that the

ABOVE

63rd Primetime Emmys®
Governors Ball floral
achitecture

Nadine Froger Photography

©ATAS/NATAS

performers were alive, for the next 45 minutes Cloris improvised, danced and mimed right along with them, to the delight of 200 photo-snapping guests but completely blocking my main exit, and much to the chagrin of the fire marshal.

"Cloris," I said to her, when I was finally able to escort her to her table. "You are a complete hit. Promise me you'll come back next week."

Considering safety as well as aesthetics, the venue, fire marshal, technicians, and I had agreed that our monstrous sea anemone chandeliers would hang no lower than 10 feet off the floor, out of reach of even the most rambunctious revelers. As they undulated, spun, elevated, and descended over the crowd, their thousands of beads twinkled under the dozens of white lights that Ray Thompson—Images by Lighting's brilliant lighting designer—had carefully focused in their direction. During the first portion of the evening, the anemone chandeliers sparkled in shimmering white light and psychedelic projections. As the evening moved on towards the finale, they suddenly reflected the entire rainbow, as the light was transformed from white to multi-colored. Warhol and Cousteau would have been proud. The lighting for each anemone was operated manually from a tech booth in a corner of the ballroom. I thought the chandeliers were a particular triumph.

Two hours into the evening, Andrea Brooks, the Governors Ball Project Manager, and I were admiring one of the larger anemones as it crept downward towards a well-populated lounge. Andrea has held the position of Project Manager for the Ball for several years and she is instrumental in its success. She is a detail person, brilliant at checks and balances and keeping an eye on sea anemones. Rather than ascending back to the ceiling, this particular anemone continued its downward crawl.

"Anemone number three! Anemone number three!" Andrea called frantically on the radio. "It's five feet off the ground. It's four feet off the ground! Guys! Guys!" The guests below, finally noticing the undersea assault, were ultimately leaning completely horizontally on their settees, desperately attempting not to spill their champagne. Gratefully, I noticed that most of them were laughing.

The boys in the booth finally answered back, "Sorry, ladies, technical issue," which I suspect might well have been code for "asleep at the wheel". From three feet off the ground, to our enormous relief, the anemone inched its way back from whence it came. To be fair, the boys in the booth were manually managing several anemones at various spots in the room, all intentionally at varying phases of their movement. I was consoled by the fact that my intrepid anemone had posed no literal threat to the guests, hanging securely from points at each end and constructed of lightweight suspended beads. I nevertheless trotted over to pour champagne all around, explaining the snafu with aplomb and ensuring that those guests would eventually depart with a humorous, undersea anecdote to tell, rather than being miffed by their close call with the décor.

Our faithful Television Academy CFO, Frank Kohler signed off letting the band go into overtime, and we danced the night away.

I'm Going to Disneyland

MISSING MOUSEKETEERS

Yep, I rehearse. I rehearse everything. I was an actress, now I'm a producer, so I rehearse even more. I leave nothing to chance.

Sometimes the world has other ideas.

A live special event is preceded by meticulously timed, scheduled rehearsals. Specific acts rehearse one after the other, all day (and sometimes, all night). Presenters run through their speeches, walk-ons and walk-offs. Video and audio is run and tested, and stagehands are put through their paces. To facilitate rehearsal, there are schedules, call times, wake-up calls, limo pick-ups and a myriad more things to be done.

One year at the G'DAY USA Black Tie Gala, the featured Australian indigenous performers, headed by the marvelous didgeridoo player, Richard Walley, failed to show up for their rehearsal. The clock was ticking. This was their only opportunity to rehearse with the music, lighting, and sound all cued up. We called them. No answer. We called their reps out of bed in Australia, who had no information and who I'm sure went soundly back to sleep. Our 9 a.m. to 11 p.m. rehearsal came and went. No sign. We reconvened on the afternoon of the Gala to quickly realign the show without the act. The show would survive, though I was desperately concerned at this point that they were alright, wherever they were. They had flown from Down Under. Where on earth could they be?

That night, the show was well into its first act, the dancers, singers, movie clips, presenters and recipients all appearing and/or performing like clockwork. Approximately 30 minutes before they were scheduled to perform, the missing dance troupe appeared at the back of the ballroom through a guest entrance, completely costumed (which is really more body paint than clothing), holding their Aboriginal props, including large, carved wooden didgeridoos. They appeared quite lost. A waiter had the presence of mind to introduce himself, and then walked the disparate group over to me. I was sitting in the tech booth directing the show. Over the show radio, we frantically wrote their set back into the show. I hustled them across the room (remember that ballroom run that doesn't look like running?), and handed them over to the stage manager. Almost immediately, they performed their set. Flawlessly. It appeared to me that they thought the whole thing was normal. The audience had no idea. I had aged five years.

"That was wonderful!" I exclaimed when I met the group after their performance. "Bravo! So, where were you?" I asked them, quite pointedly. "We had no idea you would be here because you weren't at rehearsal yesterday! We called! I was so worried," I said, sounding more like the proverbial stage mother than a producer.

"Oh," one of the dancers answered, his eyes beaming. "We've never been to the U.S. before, so we decided to go to Disneyland!"

Well, why not? Disneyland is the "Happiest Place on Earth".

This recipe uses a classic French chicken velouté scented deliciously with winter black truffles. You may substitute or add to the vegetables we've used below according to your taste, however, please do make sure anything added to the velouté mixture is as dry as possible. A vegetarian version of this can be made by substituting vegetable or mushroom stock for chicken stock in the velouté recipe and by adding more vegetables in place of the chicken.

Wolfgang Puck's Truffled Chicken Pot Pie

INGREDIENTS

2 cups cooked pearl onions

2 cups cooked baby carrots, sliced into rings

2 cups cooked (or defrosted if frozen) green peas

18 slices black truffle

Meat from the chicken cooked in the stock

Puff pastry cut into circles that overlap your ramekin or
   vessel by 1½ in. (4 cm)

Flour for dusting

2 whole eggs +1 egg yolk, for egg wash

Enriched Chicken Stock

1 gallon (4.5 litres) chicken stock

3–3½ lb (1.4–1.6 kg) whole chicken

1 carrot, peeled and chopped

2 stalks celery, chopped

2 yellow onions, peeled and chopped

3 sprigs thyme

1 bay leaf

Chicken Velouté

½ cup (4 oz/115 g) butter

½ cup (2 oz/60 g) plain (all-purpose) flour

2 pints (1.1 litres) enriched chicken stock

1 cup (8 fl oz/250 ml) crème fraîche

2 tablespoons black truffle oil

¼ cup chopped black truffle

1 lemon

Salt (or truffle salt), to taste

White pepper, to taste

SERVES 6

METHOD

For the enriched chicken stock

1. Combine all the ingredients in a large stockpot and bring to a boil. Reduce the heat to bring the liquid to a simmer and continue to simmer for 2 hours, skimming off the fat that gathers regularly. Remove the chicken and set aside. Strain the enriched stock through a fine mesh sieve and skim any remaining fat off the top. Reserve 2 pints (1.1litre) for the velouté and freeze the rest for later use in a soup or sauce.

For the Chicken velouté

1. Make a roux by melting the butter in a pan over gentle heat. Once completely melted, whisk in the flour. Cook over low heat for 5 minutes while continually whisking. Slowly add the enriched stock to the roux. Bring the velouté to a boil and then reduce the heat to low and simmer the sauce for 5 minutes. Velouté should be slightly thick. Strain through a fine mesh sieve. Add truffle oil, crème fraîche and chopped truffle. Whisk thoroughly, season to taste with salt and pepper and lemon juice. Check for consistency. Make sure it's not too thick, loosen with more stock if necessary. Leave to cool.

To prepare the pot pie

1. Preheat the oven to 350°C/180°F.
2. In a large bowl, combine the velouté, vegetables, and chicken and mix well.
3. Spoon the mixture into 4 in. (10 cm) wide deep ramekins, leaving space at the top of each. Place 3 slices of shaved truffle on top of the mixture in each ramekin.
4. On a lightly floured surface, roll out the puff pastry, then cut out rounds slightly larger than the diameter of the ramekins.
5. To make an egg wash, whisk the eggs and egg yolk together in a bowl.
6. Brush the edge of the ramekins with egg wash and inside the rim. Cover each ramekin with a puff pastry round and secure by pressing the edge around the outside of the ramekin. Brush with egg wash. Bake until golden brown (20–23 minutes), glazing again with egg wash halfway through cooking.

Recipe courtesy of the amazing Matt Bencivenga,
Chef and Managing Partner, Wolfgang Puck Catering

CHAPTER 6

Some of My Favorites

Runway Buffet

GUESS WHAT?

It's occasionally a challenge to convince my colleagues and vendors that a concept will succeed. Once I imagine an idea, I don't let it go until I give it a try. I also can't imagine it not working. I just look my colleagues square in the eyes and say, "We just have to do it. It will work." It's my responsibility to communicate my ideas as succinctly as I can, so everyone involved can imagine it together. Whatever seemingly wacky idea I come up with, faithful craftsmen build it, technicians suspend it, and lighting designers light it. Everyone's common goal is that the event succeeds. I need everyone not only to be on board, but also to be enthusiastic. In truth, it doesn't always work exactly as I expect or had imagined, but 90 percent of the time, we prevail. Nothing and no one is perfect.

Sequoia produced a high profile 20th anniversary party for Guess®, the contemporary clothing chain. Paul Marciano, Co-Founder of Guess—a man of exquisite taste, and my client for the project—heads the company's marketing department. Paul's knowledge and affection for his brand is phenomenal. Through the use of their signature award-winning advertising campaigns, Guess has inspired the style of two generations and transformed many unknown faces into famous models. Today, Guess is a global lifestyle brand with a full range of apparel and accessories sold in more than 80 countries.

For the overall décor of this event, I listened intently to Paul's inspiring ideas. Together we planned color combinations and accessories from a culture not typically familiar to Western guests. Our Moroccan theme with its draped fabrics, antique carpets, aged wood furniture, and gold and silver table and floor props afforded plenty of spice and drama. I took full advantage of draping queen extraordinaire, Daryl Latter's fabric skills, resulting in a fantastical Moroccan fairytale. Bruce Rubenstein, an incredible visual artist, was hired to paint a stunning faux-finish runway.

The runway was a critical element of the design, which would be used to host a snazzy fashion show finale, once the guests had mixed, mingled, wined and dined. The fashion show was to set an upbeat, exhilarating tone, full of movement.

With Busby Berkeley flair, I conspired to commandeer the catwalk as soon as the fashion show had delivered its stunning finish. As the models exited, we planned for African drummers to appear immediately from numerous entrances to the room, accompanied by Cirque du Soleil-esque gymnasts, weaving through the guests. During this cacophony of distraction, dancers would sprint down the runway trailing long waves of fabric. Via two doors from the kitchen, 20 tuxedoed waiters would appear, then 40, then 80, walking in military unison, to place 80 tiered trays of desserts on the fabric just as it settled on the runway platform. The whole transformation would take three minutes.

Wolfgang Puck's management voiced concern that if the waiter choreography failed, they would carry the blame. "It's not that we don't love your idea to death, Cheryl, but these are waiters. We want to serve dessert, not wear it on our faces." I heard them, loud and clear.

Over the years, I have learned to listen. Listening was definitely not one of my trademark characteristics when I first started out in the business. So I sat and listened to the captains and their concerns. I listened to the fact that they really needed to handle what they do best: service and food.

"This is impossible. This is not what we do," management chimed in.

I replied, "It is what your people do. Most of them are actors, actresses, and dancers. They can do this. Don't worry, I'll block out an hour of rehearsal in the production schedule. We are going to spike (place tabs of tape on the ground) our starting line and our final positions. The sounds of the drums will lead the waiters' parade. We will rehearse until all are comfortable, I promise."

An "hour of rehearsal" translates into more dollars and cents. I went back to Paul Marciano. He loved the idea of theatrically flipping the runway into dessert, in front of everyone. I said to him, "Like anything, we need to rehearse the waiters. I need an hour more of Wolfgang's waiters' time to make this work."

In his beautiful French-Moroccan accent, Paul replied, "Che-rille, what does that mean?"

It equated to about $5,000, and he said, "Fine, Che-rille!" Simple as that.

I ran the rehearsal like an over-enthusiastic high school drama teacher. "Places people. Okay, please memorize who is at your left and right. On the final two beats of the drums, everyone turn in unison to face the runway. This is our final position. Perfect. Let's start from the top." I'm sure everyone had had an earful from me and then some, by the time we finally opened the doors.

The changeover to dessert was flawless. How often does dessert receive a standing ovation without actually being lit on fire? (Which, perhaps, I would have done, if the fire marshal had let me. Maybe next time!)

ABOVE

Guess® 20th Anniversary Celebration entryway

Nadine Froger Photography

The Stars Come Out

HOLLYWOOD AND HIGHLAND

At the turn of the new millennium, the Kodak Theatre and Ballroom (now the Dolby Theatre) at the Hollywood and Highland Complex was designed and built specifically to "bring the Oscars® back to Hollywood". Hollywood Boulevard was still there, of course, with many of its iconic buildings intact, but it was no longer the center of the entertainment industry, nor was it where the industry gathered and celebrated.

Sequoia was hired to produce the Hollywood and Highland Grand Opening. Four thousand were expected to attend. I toured the facility, especially intrigued by the front entrance, christened "Awards Walk", a large hallway framed by a three story high proscenium, set back from the sidewalk, complete with equally magnificent drapery. On Oscar night, Hollywood Boulevard would transform into the red carpet, as guests make their way to Awards Walk and on into the Oscar telecast. Rob Reiner and Anjelica Huston, multi-generation Hollywood royalty, and Randy Newman had all agreed to appear.

I suggested to my team, "Well, it's a grand opening and it's the new venue for the Oscars celebration. Let's really open it, theater style!" We hired and choreographed 50 Rockette-inspired, male and female dancers, —the men in black-and-white formal attire with top hats and tails, and the ladies' outfits complete with fishnet stockings and high heels.

We were not given "ownership" of the boulevard until midnight the night before, necessitating an overnight installation, managed by my niece, Sasha Bruno. It was a thrill, I must say, for a Canadian to close down Hollywood Boulevard in order to install lighting, sound, hidden confetti cannons and guest seating for a big Hollywood opening. A particular delight for me was our inspired stage for the dancers and speakers and for Mr. Newman's performance. Constructed with a metal framework, black fabric and acrylic, the stage was assembled in two large pieces, and on wheels. It was self-supporting and fastened together with industrial-strength latches.

The show was terrific. Randy Newman sang *I Love L.A.*, Rob Reiner officiated, and Anjelica Huston spoke eloquently. The magnificent AME Gospel Choir sang *America The Beautiful*. We wept. Upon the final fanfare, 20 cannons blasted confetti into the air from all directions, including nearby rooftops. The top hat dancers gracefully separated the two halves of the stage, pulling it along its wheels to the left and right, revealing Awards Walk. At that exact moment, 30 additional dancers rolled out the red carpet through the separated stage, through the audience, and across Hollywood Boulevard to the opposite curb. The top hat dancers beckoned the guests to enter the building. Hollywood was reborn.

OPPOSITE PAGE

Hollywood & Highland
Grand Opening Illustration
Rendering by Luis Blanc
Courtesy of Rockwell Group
Oscar Statuette ©A.M.P.A.S.®

The Shape of a Woman

In September 2009, the Academy of Motion Picture Arts and Sciences called to inform me that the Ball Chair position for the 2010 Ball was assigned to Jeffrey Kurland, an Academy Governor and now a Vice President. Jeffrey is a prolific, Oscar®-nominated costume designer, winner of the BAFTA Best Costume Design Award for *Radio Days* and the Costume Designers Guild Award for *Erin Brockovich*. His appointment to the position constituted a huge change for me as I had formed a wonderful working relationship and dear friendship with the previous Ball Chair of several years, Cheryl Boone Isaacs, now President of the Academy.

The Academy scheduled our first Committee meeting at Hollywood and Highland. Of course, in wishing to make a good first impression, in front of an award-winning costume designer, I changed my mind five or six times while figuring out what I was going to wear.

At the appointed time I strode into the meeting prepared to pitch an extremely futuristic, cutting-edge design. Jeffrey listened very quietly; not a good sign. When I was done, he said simply, "No. I'd really love to bring more of an organic, sensual look to the Ball," and then began describing his ideas inspired by a woman's body and gesturing the shapes and curves as he spoke. I scribbled ever so quickly. Jeffrey's plan for the room included only rounded edges in various forms and directions, and no hard angles. I left the meeting with my ego a little deflated, but that was fine. I was already excited about Jeffrey's ideas and brainstorming how I could support and drive his vision.

Art and architecture bookstore, Hennessey and Ingalls, is one of my favorite pit stops to browse and daydream. I dropped in on my way back to the office. At the time, I had been studying a man named Paul R. Williams, an incredible, pioneering African-American architect. Born in 1894 in Los Angeles, Williams was orphaned at the age of four. Initially discouraged by his high school architecture teacher from entering the profession, he was warned that only white clients would be in a position to hire him to build expensive houses or buildings, but would never do so. Williams persisted, completing his education. He initially worked as an architect, often for very little money, in the early 1920s. To appease skittish Caucasian clients who might be reluctant to sit next to him, he became known as the architect who could draw upside down, so that clients could sit across from him. At age 28, Williams opened his own office, and his reputation and body of work continued to grow. Eventually, he designed the homes of progressive Hollywood luminaries such as Lucille Ball, Frank Sinatra, and Tyrone Power, though he still encountered prejudice in other circles.

Williams' projects ultimately numbered more than 3,000. His design that I found particularly captivating was the original high-end department store Saks Fifth Avenue. The owner of Saks, Adam Gimbel, envisioned an inviting, comfortable space from which no one would want to leave. To that end, he commissioned a

OPPOSITE PAGE
82nd Academy Awards®
Governors Ball "cigarette girls'" costume design by
Jeffrey Kurland
Line 8 Photography

residential architect rather than a commercial one to design his store.

Photographs of Williams' ceiling treatment for Saks featured curved lines and indirect recessed lighting. They seemed quite reminiscent of a woman's body, it seemed to me, whether Williams had intended that or not. I shared a common goal with Mr. Gimbel and Jeffrey Kurland; I didn't want anyone to want to leave the Ball.

Inspired by Williams' beautiful Saks Fifth Avenue ceiling, we installed a massive, curved truss framework under the center ceiling of the ballroom. The indispensable Nelson Sosa dressed the truss with a taut fabric emulating a hard surface. Larry Oberman then designed concealed indirect lighting with all the technical support disguised. The success of any beautiful design requires that the hardware and supporting structure be concealed. The ceiling pattern was duplicated on the floor via multiple layers of detailed carpeting. The final product indeed suggested a woman's body. The staircase up to the raised orchestra traced her gentle neckline. Though the female form inspired the design, guests would never guess the inspiration. The enchanting, swirling rounded lines throughout the room also suggested infinity, as opposed to a room of fixed, finite dimensions. Teardrop, beaded fiber-optic chandeliers, in concert with the indirect lighting, highlighted the Williams-inspired design.

For the *pièce de résistance* Jeffrey dressed 15 cocktail waitresses who held custom, strapped cigarette trays—reminiscent of old Hollywood—offering guests Wolfgang Puck hors d'oeuvres. The décor gracefully emulated that of the 1930s Streamline Moderne—accented with a contemporary edge and a flavor of Dorothy Draper, whose unique and colorful designs were prevalent in hotels in the 1920s. For our guest arrival, I positioned the waiters in sweeping lines along the curves facing the door, each offering trays of bubbly. As the guests entered, new Hollywood was reacquainted with the gifted, timeless and especially courageous designs of Los Angeles pioneer Paul Williams, with a touch of Dorothy Draper added for good measure.

Roberta Karsch of Resource One adorned the tables with the most exquisite linens to accent the room, choosing each piece of fabric methodically and tastefully. It doesn't get any better than Roberta.

The massive undertaking of seating Hollywood's elite was orchestrated by Kimberly Roush, the Academy of Motion Picture Arts and Sciences' Managing Director of Membership and Awards. Thank goodness for Kimberly.

No bomb squads, no jumping fish, and no blackout. It was just beautiful, intriguing, mesmerizing, and one of my most deeply satisfying events. Hats off to you, Jeffrey, for your direction, support and trust. I think Paul Williams would have felt quite at home.

Starlight, Star Bright

THE OBSERVATORY

Perched on the slopes of Mount Hollywood, overlooking the city of Los Angeles, is the famed and beloved Griffith Observatory, an iconic building and a national leader in astronomy and the promotion of scientific research.

Almost five years in the making, the multi-million dollar renovation and expansion of this functioning observatory, museum, and treasured landmark necessitated a celebration, highlighting key elements of the museum rather than a potentially distracting event concept. The event was entitled, "Griffith Observatory Re-Opening Galactic Gala".

Gary spent many hours with our client, Kathy Schloessman, President of the Los Angeles Sports and Entertainment Commission, brainstorming a magnificent celebration that would underscore the Observatory's rich history, and current contributions to the Los Angeles community. Appropriately centered on the stars, the night would showcase the Observatory's primary function, while also pampering guests at every opportunity in "Hollywood Star" fashion. Gary's décor and service amenities were designed to connect guests with the Observatory.

Parking for 1,500 guests was simply not available near the Observatory. Rehearsed, uniformed hosts were assigned to man dozens of shuttle buses transferring guests from parking lots to the celebration. These hosts provided a brief synopsis of what was in store for the evening, generating excitement about the exhibits and presentations.

A blue carpet reflecting the sky and the cosmos guided guests toward the outdoor cocktail area. Upon arrival, "passport" booklets were provided, detailing each exhibit and event, and playfully encouraging guests to visit the entire facility that evening, as they collected decals specific to each location.

To begin, guests assembled at the face of the famed 71-year-old American institution, to be commemorated by Mayor Antonio Villaraigosa and other dignitaries. During the cocktail hour, a single star visible to the telescope was projected in real time across the face of the building. At the precise moment that the star arrived at the inside of the letter "O" in the Observatory's permanent signage, an explosion of stellar imagery, captured from outer space, illuminated the entire building with the magic and wonder of starlight. Guests were then guided inside to view scientific displays, and gaze through the telescope itself.

Strategically positioned outdoor musical performances permeated to the inside of the venue, but at a level that encouraged conversation and astronomic contemplation.

Spreads of miso salmon, pumpkin ravioli and salads were presented on food stations placed in unobtrusive locations. Chocolate fountains and full dessert buffets were located at key positions on the roof, adjacent

OPPOSITE PAGE

Griffith Observatory
Re-Opening Galactic Gala
bar among exhibits
Nadine Froger Photography

to the telescope enclosure, which encouraged guests to peer deep into the cosmos. Bars placed in nooks and crannies around the building offered whimsical, space-age signature cocktails such as Blue Moons, Watermelon Wormholes, Big Dippers, Galactic Gimlets, Planetary Punch, and Martian Mojitos.

The Observatory's own presentations included screenings of *Centered on the Universe* in the Samuel Oschin Planetarium Theater, and *The Once and Future Griffith Observatory*, a documentary hosted by Leonard Nimoy screened in the new 200-seat Leonard Nimoy Event Horizon. A photo opportunity offered guests the chance to take home a keepsake photograph of themselves, framed by the night sky.

The Griffith Observatory endures as a key tourist attraction in Southern California and as a vital, entertaining, and informational reminder of our relationship to the cosmos. It offers guided tours to children and adults alike, educating us about the remarkable world in which we live.

Gary's work is nothing short of spectacular, underscoring his tremendous talent and unwavering dedication. There's not a person on this earth who doesn't love him, including his staff, clients and his four (and counting) doting dogs. Gary's disarming South African accent contributes that extra touch of charm and eloquence that money cannot buy.

OPPOSITE PAGE
Griffith Observatory
Re-Opening Galactic Gala
dinner lounge
Nadine Froger Photography

RIGHT
Griffith Observatory
Re-Opening Galactic Gala
light show finale
Gary Leonard

PAGES 172-173
Griffith Observatory
Re-Opening Galactic Gala
"Blue Carpet" arrivals
Nadine Froger Photography

Got Mambo?

EL MOCAMBO

"No Cheryl, I don't want to separate the ballroom, east from west," announced the energetic, charming and very candid Academy of Motion Picture Arts and Sciences President, the late Tom Sherak. Tom, a widely respected film executive, possessed the intelligence and charm of a true leader. I don't know how well I disguised my shock.

"But Tom," I said, "it's a formal, sit-down dinner. The orchestra and dance floor invite guests to move and mingle. It drives the energy. The up-tempo dance band after dinner, even more so."

"I'm sorry, Cheryl. I don't want the orchestra in the center." Tom continued, "I want guests to see each other without half of the guests separated from the other half."

By the way, this was only 60 seconds into my presentation to the Academy Awards® Governors Ball Committee. I respectfully said, "Okay Tom, I hear you loud and clear. We'll come up with a plan B. No problem."

It was a problem, or at least a challenge. In my mind's eye I now saw a dance floor huddled against a wall, the guests at the furthest tables discovering that they had been relegated to another zip code. But Tom was the client, his concern about connectivity was clear. I saw his point.

Unconventional, lounge-style seating lends itself well to a dance floor placed closer to a wall because the floor plan facilitates, even encourages guest movement throughout. However, free movement is not as conducive with conventional, banquet-style sit-down seating.

In 2011, the Ball Chair once again was Jeffrey Kurland, an artist who oozes classic design, with a tip of his hat specifically to Golden Age Hollywood. Jeffrey sports a leather jacket and loves to laugh. The 2011 design emulated the iconic nightclubs of the Golden Hollywood era, The Rainbow Room and The El Mocambo. We dubbed our creation "The El Mocambo Year." I would have LOVED to live in Los Angeles during that era, as I love the glamorous shapes and the lush layering. I love to dance and that era never stopped dancing. In our case, the dancing was suddenly the challenge. As the design concept evolved, I turned my attention back to our original dilemma, that of a displaced orchestra. I was convinced that an expansive, central dance floor surrounding a rotating orchestra would invite movement, celebration and commingling. The dance floor was a necessity, but where to put the musicians? In previous years, I had often placed the orchestra stage on a 12-foot high platform over the exit doors to the balcony adjacent to the south wall, quite close to the epicenter of our rectangular ballroom, albeit one flight up. This was a very commanding location for the orchestra and would satisfy Tom's priority of an unobstructed view across the ballroom. The problem was it did not encourage dancing.

OPPOSITE PAGE

83rd Academy Awards®
Governors Ball
Line 8 Photography
Oscar Statuette ©A.M.P.A.S.®

The orchestra, raised as it was on "stilts", invited guests to stroll underneath, arriving at the fully tented and dressed balcony (though they could never guess that they were actually in a tent). Once there, guests could enjoy additional lounge seating and especially the lavish chocolate bar.

My rule of thumb; break out the chocolate whenever necessity requires guests to populate a certain area in order to utilize all spaces and prevent bottlenecks. Stroll they did. Did you know that chocolate releases serotonin and dopamine, hormones essential for the feeling of falling in love? All the more reason to include it.

With the orchestra situated, I refocused on the décor. We designed a lowered ceiling, which facilitated a conservatory-like, raised dome in the center, supported by circular truss and lit in a rainbow of hues. Layered aluminum palm fronds draped down from the center of the dome, formed a colorful, tropical pergola over the dance floor.

We included dynamic elements that altered not only the mood, but also the actual structural shapes. We suspended huge, custom-built, Swarovski crystal chandeliers at points around the dome, which could elevate and descend, depending on musical and stage cues.

We approached the perfect headliner who could raise the temperature after dinner for the high energy dance portion of the evening. Tito Puente, Jr. accepted the invitation. However, we couldn't imagine relegating Tito to a balcony platform. His Latino flair and showmanship demanded he be up close and personal with the revelers.

I devised a compromise, building a modular champagne lounge, essentially a multi-tiered and oversized ottoman with built-in cushy seating and populated with beautiful cocktail waitresses. A full-sized, El Mocambo-inspired palm tree extended upwards, reaching towards the pergola. Commanding only a small footprint, this central mini-lounge would serve to attract guests to commingle, more than it would obscure anyone's view. Jeffrey designed the cocktail ladies' stunning costumes. He couldn't have cared less that they could barely walk in their stiletto shoes. The girls were truly show-stopping. We both felt how Florenz Ziegfeld, the great Broadway impressario, must have felt next to his bevy of costumed beauties.

Our *pièce de résistance*, the champagne lounge, was built in sections and removable within seconds. We arranged to preset all of Tito's technical requirements beneath the furniture. At the precise moment that Tito would enter, the cushions and platform would be removed in rehearsed precision (you know I rehearse everything!) by about 20 traffic controllers (traffic controllers: staff who direct guests throughout the evening). The palm tree trunk would elevate majestically towards the ceiling, revealing Tito's mini-stage and sound equipment, pre-set on a smaller stage platform hidden beneath. The night of, only 10 guests noticed this quick and silent set change. Most were surprised to hear the lively downbeat of Tito's band, only to discover him in the center of the room. Our champagne sponsor could not have been more delighted, and Tom was only too happy to support the captivating theatrics. I clearly remember the Academy Executive Director Bruce Davis and his wife, Joann, standing at the side of the dance floor, glasses of champagne in hand, gazing at our centerpiece and smiling. Bruce was a man of few words, but his expression said everything.

Tom was later appointed Film Czar by Los Angeles Mayor Eric Garcetti and commissioned to reestablish the city as a superior film production location.

Hats off to you, Tom. You raised the stakes, you held our feet to the fire, and you were always an inspiration.

OPPOSITE PAGE

83rd Academy Awards®

Governors Ball

Duke Photography

Photo courtesy of Resource One

Oscar Statuette ©A.M.P.A.S.®

Diamonds are a Girl's Best Friend

99,528 OF THEM

In 2007, the Primetime Emmys® Governors Ball was bursting at the seams at its regular home, the very large Shrine Auditorium. In 2008, the Television Academy decided to move the telecast and Ball to the Nokia Theatre in downtown Los Angeles, and the monstrously-sized Los Angeles Convention Center, next door.

The Ball Co-Chairs that year were the uber-talented, Dwight Jackson and Russ Patrick. Dwight is a prolific set designer and decorator for television, theater, art and film projects. He commits himself 120 percent to all of his work. Russ is a longtime public relations wizard in the entertainment field. Among his many talents, Russ helms his company, Patrick Communications, a Hollywood staple. Russ is a fellow Canadian, so my affection for him is built right in.

I felt nothing but compassion for the fabled Goldilocks (of *Goldilocks and the Three Bears*) when I first walked into the mammoth West Hall A at the Los Angeles Convention Center. Whereas the Shrine had grown just too small, the Convention Center was just too big, thereby presenting its own challenges: 147,506 square feet of them.

An event space must fit the guest count, lest the attendees feel uncomfortably crowded together or too spread out. What would we do with more than two football fields' worth of space, short of offering champagne and rollerblades upon guest arrival? The very first Ball at the Convention Center, the Emmys 60th Anniversary to boot, mandated transforming the vast space to our best advantage.

Dwight set his sights on diamonds, as in 60th Diamond Jubilee. We chatted on the phone about Marilyn Monroe singing *Diamonds Are a Girl's Best Friend* in the 1950s film *Gentlemen Prefer Blondes*. Ever the designer at heart, Dwight took his inspiration from the countless diamonds featured in the song, as well as from Marilyn's form-fitting, pinker-than-pink dress.

One day during pre-production, Dwight called me excitedly. "Cheryl! There is this chandelier at Costco that's perfect. Let's order 300-ish. We can string bracelets of 'diamonds' flowing down from every point in the ceiling," Dwight said.

"Fantastic, Dwight," I said, "But before we order 300-ish, let's order one and see what we're in for."

A few days later, a box arrived at my office. The chandelier included 319 beautiful, conspicuously unassembled glass "crystals". We counted. I asked my team, "How long will it take us to put one of these together?" Assembling our prototype, we soon realized the answer was "… long". However, this chandelier was the one we wanted. Commitment to excellence seldom affords an easy route. These chandeliers shipped unassembled, it was as simple as that. My technicians also noticed that the wiring provided by the manufacturer to string the crystals together was not what one would describe as

OPPOSITE PAGE
60th Primetime Emmys®
Governors Ball
ascending chandeliers
Nadine Froger Photography
©ATAS/NATAS

"industrial strength". Suspending one of these chandeliers three feet above a dining room table was one thing. Suspending 312 of them 45 feet above a ballroom floor with 3,600 bullseyes (a.k.a. 3,600 guests), was quite another matter.

We rewired our prototype chandelier as we assembled it, realizing as it took shape that it wasn't possible to lay this particular glass-beaded chandelier down on a table. You learn something new every day. Once assembled, the chandeliers could only be mounted in their position, or mounted somewhere. Assembly on site, however, was out of the question, as we didn't acquire West Hall A in time to complete the assembling. During production, I couldn't afford to give up nearly enough on-site real estate that would be required to complete the job. I sleep soundly at night specifically due to my religious habit of executing EVERYTHING as much as possible in advance. There was no way around rewiring and preassembling 312 chandeliers off-site, by hand. Upright wooden boxes were designed and constructed to house each completed, hanging chandelier, all of which was accomplished in a warehouse.

For the purpose of press previews and releases, we described the crystals as hand-polished glass pendants. Doesn't that sound glamorous? I was a math wiz in high school, but basic multiplication was all I needed to know that 312 chandeliers translated into 99,528 hand-polished, glass pendants. I repeated my calculation several times and asked my assistant to give it a go as well, but the 99,528 figure persisted. I managed to resist renaming the crystals 99,528 rewired, hand assembled, hand polished, high-maintenance glass pendants.

Hats off to the brilliant Keith Greco and Stephen Mar, who spent five weeks assembling the 312 chandeliers, then five days connecting them with PVC pipe and masking the rigging.

Guests are blissfully unaware of the challenges faced by the production team to create a carefree evening of celebrating, dining, and dancing the night away. That is as it should be.

The vast raw space of West Hall A still demanded our attention. Under the artistic direction of Dwight Jackson, the Television Academy purchased 47,520 square feet of black velvet, L.E.D. (light emitting diodes) custom-made star-field drapery. The glowing stars formed 15 giant constellation patterns, multiplied four times, ultimately encompassing the entire circumference of the room and reducing it to the exact, desirable size for our guest count. Not too big, not too small, but just right.

Once again, with the Sequoia "every seat is a VIP seat" rule in mind, we decided to build wide platforms on the floor in the four corners of the room, equipped with staircases and railings, that raised guest seating towards the corners up to three and five foot levels. These vantage points afforded expansive views of the room, while also suggesting a feeling of sequestered VIP areas. From the center of the room, the raised seating in the corners suggested a reverse curvature of the earth. The floor-to-ceiling, black star-field drapery surrounding the ballroom disappeared into the infinity once we directed our lights onto the ballroom itself. We ultimately dubbed our encompassing black drapery "infinity walls".

During pre-production, the sheer magnitude of the figures passing across my desk in various requisitions and invoices prompted me to check in with my vendors for some numbers, and then release a staggering list of statistics, a.k.a. "fun facts" for the public:

- 3,600 guests
- 450 waiters
- 85 managers
- 45 bartenders
- 177 chefs in the kitchen
- 75 chefs for five days of pre-production
- 10,800 pieces of china
- 20,000 pieces of assorted glassware (even I have trouble wrapping my head around that number, but the rental order does not lie)
- 160 yards of pink curtain fabric adorning the chandelier installation
- 2,000 yards of black velvet adorning the flower containers
- 500 yards of rhinestones for the same purpose
- 360 bottles of Piper-Heidsieck champagne
- 1,560 bottles of assorted Beaulieu Vineyard vintage wines (Heaven)

In deference to Marilyn Monroe, we included pink, mid-century-style lounges surrounding the guest tables. Pink and diamond accenting infiltrated our entire set. I realized on the night that our many tuxedoed waiters serendipitously mimicked Marilyn's dancers. I'd like to think that Marilyn would have spent the whole night in the lounge, sipping bubbly with Andy Warhol and entertaining her admirers, perhaps bursting into her famous *Diamond's Are a Girl's Best Friend*, too.

My favorite "fun fact" of all:

- 25,000 stems of pink roses. Yes, I lugged a few dozen up to my hotel room after all was said and done. We encouraged every departing waiter to indulge in as many roses as they could carry.

As the night drew to a close, I realized that diamonds really are a girl's best friend. Congratulations to my crazy, fabulous friends, Dwight and Russ.

PAGE 182-183
60th Primetime Emmys®
Governors Ball
Craig Mathew
Photos courtesy of the
Television Academy
©ATAS/NATAS

My Favorite Moment

DREAMING OF ALEX

My favorite moment? That's easy…

In 2011, Sequoia Productions was honored to produce the Black Tie Gala Fundraiser "Dream for Kids". This was one of the opening festivities commemorating the Children's Hospital Los Angeles' magnificent, state-of-the-art new patient tower, set in the heart of the city. The event honored Marion Anderson, Chris Albrecht, and Mary Hart—selfless Children's Hospital Los Angeles champions—and ultimately raised an unprecedented one billion dollars for medical research and children's care.

Fabricated in an enormous tent structure atop entertainment complex L.A. Live, the gala stage featured a proscenium of multicolored and stylized butterflies, the hospital's official symbol of youth and hope. Moving, three-dimensional clouds were projected on the entire ceiling above 1,500 guests. The clouds evolved into a dynamic presentation of motion picture images, including thousands of butterflies fluttering in harmony with the performance.

Meghan Gudelsky was my line producer in the show. She is a dynamo, her organization and dedication is exemplary. We just kept going, coordinating the logistics of a 200-member cast.

Eric Stonestreet of *Modern Family* assumed the role of MC; headliner Diane Krall crooned; and the evening was accented with youth-driven performances by the Debbie Allen Dance Academy, opera and acting students from the Los Angeles High School for the Arts, and the Los Angeles Youth Orchestra. Patti Austin sang the show's finale, *The Power of The Dream*.

One of our most important challenges was to locate the ideal patient story to fully illustrate the dedication and vital work of the hospital and its staff, and personify the miracles that occur there. Perusing through countless profiles, I considered many moving stories of courageous candidates. My clients provided me with the telephone number of a brave 11-year-old boy by the name of Alexander.

Alex was born with VACTERL syndrome. He endured his first surgery before he was six months old. This affliction would have threatened the growth of Alex's lungs and ribs, were it not for a miraculous new medical procedure, ultimately providing him with a custom-made titanium rib cage. For the following 10 years, Alex underwent surgery every six to nine months. By the time he was 10, he was strong enough to undergo a full spinal fusion operation. By age 11, he was enjoying middle school with his peers.

I called the family and made arrangements to meet Alex. The next day, after an hour's drive, I was sitting in the living room of the family's home. Searching for a way to introduce Alex to the audience and public, I chatted with this sincere, shy boy about what he liked to do.

"I like video games," he said.

"Really?" I asked. "I don't know much about video games. What else?"

Alex quietly added, "… and tap dancing".

"Aha!" I said. "I have an idea."

On the night of the Gala, my heart overflowed as Alex took the stage in his pressed tuxedo and made his way to the podium, much as every other presenter and recipient had done before him, though, for Alex, with many more steps. We had recorded lively play-on music, but instead of going to the podium, Alex commenced to tap dance around it. The audience cheered. Alex and I had agreed that I would fade out the music after 15 seconds, and he would step up to the podium. The audience continued to cheer, so I let the music play, and Alex continued to dance. The 15-second mark came and went, then 30 seconds. Alex was lapping it up. Apparently this little showman knew all about "giving the audience what they want." Thirty seconds went by, then 45…

At 60 seconds, the audience finally settled, and I faded out Alex's music. He stepped up to the podium. Upon gazing up at the podium mic, far above him, he snapped his fingers and called out, "Props please?"

Alex's beaming father entered stage right, carrying an apple box. Placing the box ceremoniously behind

the podium, his father exited. Alex stepped up, leaned into the microphone, and introduced himself.

"Hello, my name is Alex. I'm eleven years old." He continued with a beaming smile, "I have titanium ribs, and I've had over 27 operations. Oh and I loooove to tap dance!"

That was it. The crowd roared, with not a dry eye left in the house. Alex was a hit, with his infectious, positive demeanor shining forth like a beacon. He had personified the true spirit of the evening and the hospital itself.

Billy Crystal followed Alex, stepping up to the podium to ask "Where's my apple box?" and he continued, "By the way, Alex will be hosting the Academy Awards® next year."

The evening was packed with heartfelt speeches and performances, underscoring the spirit of a very special hospital that offers so much hope. But Alex had stolen the show and all of our hearts.

ABOVE
Children's Hospital Los
Angeles Dream for Kids Gala
performace by Los Angeles
County School for the Arts
musicians
Line 8 Photography

PAGE 188-189
Children's Hospital Los
Angeles Dream for Kids Gala
Line 8 Photography

Blowing in the Wind

BUBBLES OF INSPIRATION

The 80th Anniversary of the Academy Awards® Governors Ball was my 19th year producing. Sid Ganis was the Academy President that year and Cheryl Boone Isaacs was the Ball Chair. The future would also witness Cheryl elected as President of the Academy of Motion Picture Arts and Sciences. What an honor to work by their sides for several years—both together and separately. Isn't it incredible how one's title can create a state of anxiety in another… meaning me. Sid's position as a Hollywood producer and Cheryl's as a publicity and marketing tsar, both definitely stopped me in my tracks. Fast forward, years later, I know from so many first hand experiences, Cheryl and Sid are two of the most down to earth and supportive leaders—only a phone call away.

On a Saturday afternoon, early fall, I had brought my friend Sue, whose health was failing, out of her house and into the fresh air of the park. My son, Milan, was with us. Milan coming into a room is like turning on a light. He's a gem with an incredibly loving, calming energy. I wanted Sue to feel that. It's terrible to admit that I was squeezing in three or four hours to spend with Sue, but that's my life. Squeeze in we must, because life goes by so fast—in Sue's case, too fast.

It was a very sunny afternoon and we had prepared some fabulous food for a picnic, but Sue was very ill and the three of us felt melancholy. There were pauses in the conversation. Milan was lying on the blanket, gazing upward, his head resting on my leg. Together we noticed a twinkling of light floating past. Our eye caught several shiny bubbles, perfectly round, floating by in the sunlight. I turned my head to find a little girl, perhaps three years old, blowing bubbles. It was the simplest thing.

I said, "Sue. Look."

As the bubbles floated and bounced in the breeze, our spirits lifted. At times the little girl was completely enveloped in the clouds of bubbles she was creating. They floated and danced all around her, popping wherever and whenever they pleased. Lifting her arms she'd run alongside them, as if she were a bubble herself. The three of us watched, enraptured. In spite of, or perhaps because of, that particularly sad day, I was distracted and then inspired by the make-believe world this little girl had created.

I don't know if you've blown bubbles since pre-school, but I hadn't. The next day, I went out, bought some bubbles, and blew them off my front stoop through the little pink plastic wand. I noticed that I felt like a child again, and I giggled. My imagination was up to something.

I thought to myself, "How about bubbles floating above the Governors Ball, with focused light directed through and between, just like those magic bubbles in the park, shining under the afternoon sunlight?" They must appear as if from nowhere, unrestrained, just as we had noticed the bubbles in the park before we saw

OPPOSITE PAGE

80th Academy Awards®
Governors Ball

Nadine Froger Photography

Oscar Statuette ©A.M.P.A.S.®

the girl who was blowing them. Hmmm… we can hang them on clear monofilament, whimsical and varying in size… And off I went. I put out calls to my technical contacts and creative team.

Sequoia's own Lauren Ashamalla served as project manager for the Ball. Compared to building a house, Lauren's project manager position would correspond to the role of the "contractor", or in film, the "line producer". She started as my assistant, as did many of the Sequoia team. Lauren took off and soared, never looking back. Lauren is now fully exploring motherhood with two very lucky kids. I am so fortunate that she returns to Sequoia as often as she can to spearhead specific projects.

Lauren loved the bubble idea.

"Lauren," I said, "How the heck are we going to find and deal with all of these bubbles? We'll need thousands of them."

Lauren is my kind of person. She dives in. She'll do the research, go online, send emails, and ask questions. Lauren took the bubble and ran with it. "I got this, Cheryl."

Soon bubbles of various shapes, sizes and materials started to show up at the office. Everyone was on board, researching bubbles: my employees, my vendors, and even my housekeeper. FedEx packages from East L.A. and as far as India began to arrive. Friends of mine, having got wind of the bubble quest, surprised me with white and clear glass globes as Christmas ornaments. I was bubble obsessed and bubble inundated. But the bubbles were never quite right. "This bubble is too heavy. This bubble is not translucent."

Lauren located Lucite bubbles via an exporter from China. They were lightweight, unbreakable, available in various sizes, and the price was right. Sold.

The bubbles needed testing. At Russ Draeger's warehouse in Downtown L.A. (Russ is a rigger who physically installs sets and large pieces of hardware), Nelson Sosa drilled holes into the sides of our test bubbles in order to apply the monofilament on which they would be strung. We tested the bubbles, "floating" a group of assorted sizes from the ceiling. Our lighting company illuminated them with focused and diffused light of various colors and moving patterns.

There we all were, riggers, lighting designers, Lauren and myself, gazing heavenward. We stood very still. Our bubbles, interspersed between firefly lights, assumed the impression of being kissed by the sun. We paused under the glow, enchanted by one little girl's imagination brought to life on a grand scale.

"This is going to be good," I said. It also reminded me of celebratory bubbles of champagne, which no party should be without.

A wonderful aspect of working with the Academy of Motion Picture Arts and Sciences is that they let me run with ideas, because they strive for the cutting edge as much as I do. So I ran. I wanted 10,000 bubbles, but I think we ultimately suspended 4,000 (there's always a budget). They were transformative and transcending.

Throughout the evening of the Ball I kept thinking, "Sue, here's a little magic for you."

OPPOSITE PAGE
80th Academy Awards®
Governors Ball Press Preview
with Ball Chair
Cheryl Boone Isaacs and
Chef Wolfgang Puck
©A.M.P.A.S.

PAGE 194-195
80th Academy Awards®
Governors Ball
Nadine Froger Photography
Oscar Statuette ©A.M.P.A.S.®

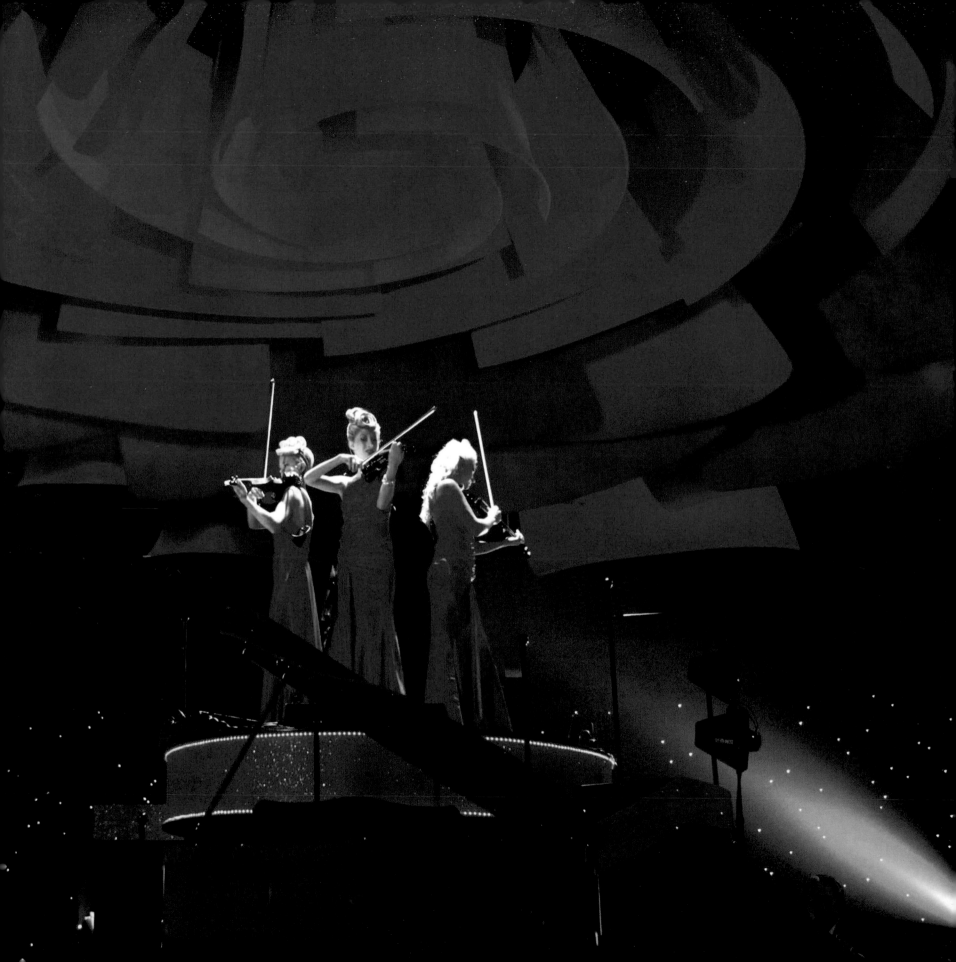

Valentino

"Process" is the connective tissue between an original idea and its final, practical execution. The initial brainstorm is followed by a number of exploratory actions, resulting in a number of options on how to proceed, as well as illuminating other notions which turn out to be impractical or unnecessary. Through process, the original brainstorm evolves and morphs dramatically. Determination and resourcefulness, not rigidity, merge with natural selection. This creativity ultimately renders the final product. Guests experience only the result, as it should be. However the producers, designers and builders behold not only the result, but the entire evolution from concept to fruition.

The 2012 Primetime Emmys® Governors Ball Chairs comprised of Joe Stewart, Geriann McIntosh, and the late Leslie Frankenheimer. At our first meeting, Joe said one word to us: "Red!"

My original rendering for the committee, extrapolating on the single, provocative word, will never again see the light of day. I'm quite certain I destroyed all traces of it long ago. This first rendering burst forth as a hanging-from-the-ceiling hodgepodge of shredded, interlocking draped fabric, vintage chandeliers, rotating lighting, red projections, and birdcages… including the birds. Resembling a scene from one of my husband's horror movie scripts, it was the culmination of what I call "monkey brain".

When I live in my right-brain for a week, I forget my keys here and my cellphone there, and once I do find my keys, I don't drive as safely as I should because I am deep in thought; that's monkey brain.

Joe was so sweet. "Okay, Cheryl. Great. Fabulous… we aren't there yet."

Joe and I looked in each other's eyes, and I agreed with him 110 percent. I decided I would conduct a survey.

"If I said the word 'red' to you, what's the first thing that comes to mind?" I asked colleagues in my working world, as well as friends and family.

Roses, was by far the most frequent response. The second most common answer was red lips, and the third, fire.

"Okay," I replied. "What do you feel when a dozen roses arrive at your doorstep?"

Everybody's answer was, "I feel that somebody loves me."

The answers were so consistent and, frankly, moving, that I realized how much the rose is loaded with emotional and metaphoric significance. We decided that the entire project concept would emanate from the romantic and fiery beauty of the red rose.

I had happened to travel home to Sudbury that particular weekend. I changed planes at Toronto International Airport—what is it about airports and ideas? Perhaps, when I fly, I'm forced to slow down and I'm more receptive? Unfortunately, catching up on work with increasingly available, onboard Wi-Fi is ending

OPPOSITE PAGE

64th Primetime Emmys®
Governors Ball

Nadine Froger Photography

the "slowing down" part. Nevertheless, at the airport I stumbled upon an art exhibit entitled *Tilted Spheres* by the artist Richard Serra. He is an American minimalist known for his large-scale sheet metal work. This particular exhibit consisted of four huge, steel fins, each delicately curved, torqued, and coated in black rust inhibitor. The information plaque indicated they were 39 feet long by 14 feet high. The four majestic, towering shapes, set on the ground, allowed travelers to walk through and around, immersing themselves. They reminded me of gigantic petals. Bingo! We could invert and suspend Richard Serra-inspired petals at the center of the ceiling, duplicating expanding segments outward in all directions. We would build a commanding rose centerpiece in the sky like no other.

While presenting our grand design to the Committee and generating collective excitement, Leslie Frankenheimer, an elegantly artistic set designer and decorator, turned to the group and said simply, "That is a Valentino rose."

The name said it all. I think the name "Valentino" influenced the theme for me as much as the word "Red", conjuring images of the work of Valentino, the designer, but also Rudolph Valentino, the movie star and "great lover" of the 1920s. Thank you, Leslie, such a generous and loving soul, and taken from us much too early.

The mammoth West Hall A of the Los Angeles Convention Center dictates larger-than-life set pieces for the best effect. Elements of any design in a space that large must anchor from a central point, focusing the energy, then expanding it to all corners— leaving no one abandoned at the periphery.

I described our inverted Valentino rose to Irma Hardjakusumah and the technical team who have faithfully brought to life every outrageous idea I've ever thrown at them. We wanted our centerpiece rose to emulate the power of the Richard Serra inspiration, yet also radiate the fragile elegance of a rose. I also suggested incorporating various textured red materials and fabric to add depth and dimension.

The rose rendering depicts a section elevation, demonstrating how it related to the stage and to the width and length of the room. Three alternating red fabrics: velvet, Lycra, and sequin-embellished, each incorporated on separate "petals", added contrast and depth. The actual 3D-artist rendering represents the 120-foot-diameter Valentino centerpiece. Assorted shades of red were used to decorate table linens, chair covers, cocktails, oh… and so many roses.

In terms of inspiration, design and construction, an event of this magnitude is comparable to a film production. Every detail, macro and micro, is meticulously chosen and crafted by artisans of varied creative specialties before somebody important gives the go-ahead. The significant difference is that when our doors open, we only get one take.

The Emmys consists of two distinct awards presentations, separated by a week. One hundred thousand red roses were incorporated into the floral arrangements for each evening: that is more than two-dozen roses per guest each night. The red roses radiated majesty, fire and romance all at once. One hundred and fifty female waitresse wore red lipstick for the occasion and all took home armfuls of roses that night, as did I, once the evening was at a close. Ultimately, I think everyone did feel loved.

Joachim Splichal's Heirloom Tomato Salad

INGREDIENTS

Asparagus

4 x 4 in. (10 cm) lengths of asparagus, peeled

1 sprig of fresh rosemary, roughly chopped

1 fl oz (30 ml) olive oil

Pinch of sea salt

Pinch of freshly ground black pepper

Tomatoes

3 large tomatoes, cut into ¼ in. (5 mm) slices

8 oz (225 g) baby tomatoes, halved

1 fl oz (30 ml) extra virgin olive oil

Potato Salad

16 Fingerling potatoes

4 fl oz (125 ml) crème fraîche

2 tablespoons Dijon mustard

2 tablespoons red onions, grilled (broiled)

Fried Potatoes

1 large potato

Pinch of sea salt

Pinch of freshly ground black pepper

SERVES 4

METHOD

For the asparagus

1. Mix the asparagus with the olive oil and rosemary.
2. Place the asparagus on a hot grill (broiler) and grill until cooked through.
3. Cut in half lengthwise and season with sea salt and ground black pepper.

For the tomatoes

1. Season the tomatoes and baby tomatoes with sea salt, ground black pepper and drizzle with extra virgin olive oil.

For the potato salad

1. Place the Fingerling potatoes in a pan of cold water and bring to a boil. Simmer until cooked through. Place under cold running water and when cool enough to handle, peel the potatoes. Slice in half lengthwise.
2. In a bowl, mix the sliced potatoes with crème fraîche, Dijon mustard and the grilled red onions. Season with sea salt and ground black pepper.

For the fried potatoes

1. Peel the potato and cut into julienne strips.
2. Fry in hot oil at 375°F/190°C until golden brown and crisp. Season with sea salt.
3. Divide the potato salad between 4 plates. Top with tomatoes, asparagus and fried gold potatoes.

Photo and recipe courtesy of Patina Restaurant Group

CHAPTER 7

Hobnobbing

Skin Deep

BEAUTIFUL PEOPLE

I'm often asked, when someone discovers what I do for a living, "Wow! Do you meet a lot of celebrities? Have you ever met… (fill in your favorite celebrity here)? What are they like?"

I usually reply, "So many celebrities have crossed my path, or should I say I have crossed theirs."

My joy—and responsibility—is to create a rarefied environment while supporting and enriching the client's goal. Hollywood is a very small community. Celebrity guests actually look forward to enjoying each other's company, away from the limelight. A major Hollywood fête often adopts the flavor of a festive family reunion or homecoming. Our challenge is often convincing high-profile guests to sit down for their first course, because they are so excited to reconnect with colleagues and friends. In addition, with the paparazzi and media sequestered outside, a great deal of business is actually accomplished during a large Hollywood event, with so many colleagues and associates under the same roof at one time.

I actually don't have the time to be star-struck. We have a huge responsibility and the environment is my focus, in which every person is a Very Important Person. Besides, standing next to the recognizable celebrity is often the executive who runs the whole studio and signs the paycheques, or even mine.

That said I've met some wonderful people from all walks of life. I'm moved and inspired by so many—by their generosity of heart during our time together, not by who they are, but by what they choose to give and how they choose to be of service. In the spirit of honoring so many, here are a few… but only a few.

*   *   *

I had the pleasure of working with Elle Macpherson, an "A" among A-listers, when she agreed to co-host the 2013 G'DAY USA Black Tie Gala with Australian television personality, Richard Wilkins. Once we navigated through a sea of agents, managers and riders in order to secure her, meeting Elle and working with her was an absolute delight. From start to finish, Elle was the consummate professional; focused, generous and dedicated to her contribution to the show. Her temperament was so effervescent and warm. She often assertively thanked anyone in earshot for her involvement. I was charmed by how happy Elle seemed to be, just to be there participating and having the time of her life. What a breath of fresh air. To top it off, Elle sent me the most gracious of thank you notes afterwards. She is a class act.

*   *   *

A short time after his tragic accident, Christopher Reeve attended a very high-profile event which I produced. Informed in advance about Christopher's attendance and a few special needs, I was quite honored to carry out preparations for this man who had so bravely and publicly transformed tragedy into hope when he created the Christopher and Dana Reeve Foundation.

"If it's alright, may we possibly sit in an area where we can make a quick exit, if necessary?" Christopher's camp requested in advance.

"Of course," I replied.

"Thank you so much. Is there any way we could have an electrical connection at the table?" they requested.

"Consider it done," I said.

They continued, "Just one more thing? There's a possibility we'd require a private area nearby. I'm so sorry that I'm asking so many…"

"Please say no more," I insisted. "My office is the place. I will seat you at a prime table right next to it. It's still a wonderful view of the entire room."

On the night, Christopher and his entourage were unwaveringly gracious and appreciative. Crossing paths with this inspirational man certainly puts life in perspective.

* * *

In 2005, at the annual G'DAY USA Black Tie Gala, Geoffrey Rush presented an award of distinction to Russell Crowe. Backstage, during rehearsal, I was tapped on the shoulder, and to my surprise, Geoffrey was standing in front of me, holding a sheet of paper.

"Hello, would you mind listening to my speech for Russell Crowe, and telling me what you think?" Mr. Rush and I had only first met earlier that day, for a few short moments, working out blocking and microphone levels.

"Of course," I replied. "It would be my pleasure." What I wanted to do was look around, then ask him, "Are you sure you're talking to me?"

His speech was elegant, humorous, generous, and heartfelt, as if written by an English scholar turned published poet, and of course spoken in Geoffrey's distinguished baritone. My producer's ear also noted that the speech was just the right length. Geoffrey finished, looking up at me expectantly, with tender warmth in his eyes. I melted just a little.

I paused and I simply said, "It's perfect. I wouldn't change a word. What an honor to be the first one to hear it!" In 2014, Geoffrey received his own award at the Gala and his acceptance speech just as modest and humorous as it was elegant. Later, one of my staff walked Geoffrey to an outside door where he could enjoy a breath of fresh air and make a phone call. Geoffrey said to my staff member, who was holding the award for him, "Well, this is so nice, isn't it?" as he smiled genuinely. Isn't it great when those we love on screen turn out to be so genuine and just as lovable in real life?

* * *

PAGE 206 (CONT)

Bottom row from left:

Headliner Tony Bennett at the 59th Primetime Emmys® Governors Ball

Nadine Froger Photography

Air Supply receives award at the 9th Annual G'DAY USA Black Tie Gala

Barbara Green

Judith Hill performs at the 85th Academy Awards® Governors Ball

Nadine Froger Photography

Oscar Statuette ©A.M.P.A.S.®

Back in my Ambrosia days, working for Carl Bendix and David Corwin, one of their regular clients was the adorable Paul Maslansky (most famous for producing the *Police Academy* movies) and his gracious wife, Sally. The Maslansky home was my first experience of Malibu as well as being the first party location I encountered where the expected waiter footwear was a choice between flip-flops or bare feet. We typically served sangrias on the beach, in front of the house, or to guests in the jacuzzi. I remember one day at Maslansky's, when a gentle Ed Asner, who had played the gruff and grumpy Lou Grant in the '70s television hit *The Mary Tyler Moore Show*, walked up to me and looked me square in the eye. Ed was a guest, mind you, not the host, nor the guest of honor.

"Hi, I'm Ed." He waited.

So it was my turn to say, "Oh, yes, nice to meet you, Mr. Asner. I'm Cheryl, How are you? Can I get you a drink?"

"It's Ed," he replied. "Actually, I just want to say that the food is really delicious and I really appreciate everything you've done. Thank you so much. We are having a terrific time."

Moments like that I don't forget. Now I can't watch the crotchety Lou Grant on old reruns without realizing how good an actor Ed Asner really is.

*   *   *

Quincy Jones produced the Academy Awards® telecast in 1996. Quincy has always commanded tremendous respect and wielded great power in the music and television industries, yet I've only experienced a soft voice and calm spirit whenever I've encountered him. As the telecast ended and guests arrived, I noticed Quincy entering the ballroom, appearing quite spent, as if he had just run a mile.

I sensed an opportunity to be of service. "Hello Mr. Jones, may I get you a chair and something to drink?"

"Champagne, please," he replied. "Seems appropriate." He smiled warmly.

"Of course," I said, eyeing a waiter to assist me. "How did it go?" I asked.

"That was by far the hardest thing I have ever done in my life. I thought I was going to die," he replied.

"Well, Mr. Jones, if anybody could do it, it's you," I said as I ceremoniously topped up his flute.

*   *   *

I was thrilled as soon as I heard that legends Graham Russell and Russell Hitchcock, of the Australian soft rock-and-roll band Air Supply, agreed to perform at the 2012 G'DAY USA Black Tie Gala. This band has contributed a sizable chunk of music to the soundtrack of my youth. As soon as they were booked I was quickly informed that Graham and Russell wanted to speak to me personally about the gig. It's rare when communication with a celebrity prior to performance day isn't conducted completely via a number of representatives. The duo were gracious and accommodating to a fault.

I knew that our largely Australian crowd would go ballistic as soon as Air Supply took to the stage. I envisioned a personable and charming start to their set, in which they simply rose from their tables in the ballroom, spontaneously playing among the guests as they made their way to the stage. I placed the band behind the traveler (sliding curtain) to begin the opening number. Russell, who required only a microphone, instantly agreed. Graham preferred to enter on stage, as he was holding his guitar. On the night, right on cue, a microphone was delivered and placed next to Russell's water glass a few moments before he stood under a spotlight and crooned, *"I'm all out of love…"* The crowd roared. Graham walked in from the wings and joined in.

On stage, Russell mentioned how people would ask them why they still perform, after all these years, when they could be enjoying retirement. Russell explained, "Well, as long as we still love doing it, we figure we'll keep doing it." The crowd roared again. Music for the soul, food for thought.

⋆ ⋆ ⋆

Angelina Jolie and Brad Pitt are clearly Hollywood's reigning power couple. In 2013, Angelina was honored at the Academy of Motion Picture Arts and Sciences' 4th Annual Governors Awards with the prestigious Jean Hersholt Humanitarian Award. Filming on location at that time, Angelina was flown in from overseas for the event.

Angelina spoke modestly and emotionally about how, early in her acting life, she had focused on her own feelings and career. Upon traveling a great deal to shoot on location, Angelina noticed her focus and empathy was turning towards displaced and persecuted people around the world. She discovered that her passion was to draw attention to the plight of those who are so less fortunate than us. Angelina spoke of how her mother had always supported her career without reservation. Whenever her mother witnessed a film that sought to improve the human condition, she would council Angelina, "That is what film is for."

I believe Angelina flew all that way, not only to be congratulated, but also for the opportunity to share her mother's wisdom, as well as her own resolve, to an esteemed group of influential filmmakers. I was so grateful to hear Angelina and her mother's wise words that night.

⋆ ⋆ ⋆

At the 2013 Academy Awards Governors Ball, enthusiastic headliner Michael Feinstein informed me at rehearsal, "… then at some point, Cheryl, I'm going to jump up on top of the piano."

"Oh," I replied. Acquainted with Michael's mellow recording style, this was certainly an unexpected announcement. "Okay, Michael. Good to know."

That night, after rehearsal, my technicians fixed a protective rubber mat over the top of the rented grand piano and placed a three-step staircase against it, out of the audience's line of sight. Sure enough, as his set wound up to the final number, up Michael jumped. He sang his heart out for the proverbial show stopper. Thank you, Michael. You rocked it.

* * *

Tony Bennett has performed at a number of events my company has produced. The joy and energy with which this living legend sings is astounding. Tony has played with the same dedicated musicians for decades. Well into his 80s, Tony's voice and stage presence are in top form. Invariably, people half his age and younger rush to the stage to dance to his famous music, under a sea of smart phones. Tony's fans now include a fourth generation. We should all be so lucky.

* * *

Speaking of legend, Academy of Motion Picture Arts and Sciences Chief Executive Officer, Dawn Hudson, suggested we reach out to none other than John Legend to sing at the 2014 Academy Awards Governors Ball. Dawn asked Ball Chair, Jeffrey Kurland and myself what we thought.

"I think that, well, he just went to the top of my list, I can tell you that," I said. Jeffrey agreed. Inwardly I thought, well, we can always wish.

Dawn worked her considerable magic, arranging a phone call between between us and John Legend's manager. Unlike anything I've experienced in Sequoia Productions' 25 years, we had a deal in 15 minutes.

John Legend is everything his public persona suggests. He's the sweetest guy in the world. Toward the end of his set, one couldn't move within the aisles or between the tables near the stage, as so many guests had moved towards John's piano to sing with him. He was mesmerizing. As John left the stage, he took my hand and said, "Thank you so much," and he kissed me on the cheek.

No, I don't have a crush on John Legend, but I do have a crush on his music.

* * *

A few years back, the Primetime Emmys® Governors Ball was in full swing. Word came that one of our 1,650 guests wanted to talk to me: singer-songwriter Seal.

"Seal wants to talk to me?" I asked.

"Yes, Seal," my assistant repeated.

"Okay, no problem," and we made our way to his table.

"Hello, I'm Cheryl Cecchetto, the Ball producer. How can I help you?"

"I would like to sing to my wife," he said.

"You mean, now?" I asked.

"I just promised her," he reiterated. Never a dull moment.

"Yes, that can happen, no problem." I hoped it was no problem. I hurried over to the Ball Chair, Geriann McIntosh.

"Seal wants to sing," I said.

"Well, of course!" she replied, "Can we do it?"

"Yes!" I answered, whole-heartedly.

Could we? We were very willing, but it was easier said than done: no sound check, no rehearsal, no orchestrations. Luckily, well no, intentionally, I had hired one of the best orchestras in the country, a big band conducted by Gregg Field, winner of several Latin Grammys®.

My stage manager whispered into Gregg's ear, "Seal is coming over to sing."

Gregg nodded back. Enough said.

Seal was already walking over to the stage. A guest intercepted him to say hello, which bought us precious seconds. I sprinted over to the lighting and sound booth, "Seal is going to sing," I told them.

They immediately, expertly manipulated their large, *Star Trek*-style electrical boards of hundreds of buttons and flashing lights, adding lighting, turning on microphones and adjusting speakers and reverb for the surprise headliner. A radio message was relayed to the stage turntable operator, and the orchestra platform was carefully brought to a stop, positioning the singer podium dead-center to the room. Seal took to the stage amid an improvised, dramatic lighting change, including a romantic and warm spotlight, and a grand musical flourish. Seal's performance was quite magical and quite the coup. The supposedly "planned" surprise proved a highlight of the night, as if we had intended it all along.

It was stressful for a few moments, but I had side-stepped the time and expense of all the pre-production of a headliner—no flight, no limo, no green room, no rider, no honorarium, no rehearsal, no green M&Ms, no headaches. The next day, the *Los Angeles Times* headline read, 'Emmys Governors Ball Stars Seal.' Seal stole the show. Fine with me.

*   *   *

I want to pay special tribute to two dear friends who have supported, befriended me and who I have cherished for almost two decades. I met Alan Bergman and his lovely wife and writing partner, Marilyn, many years ago when Alan was Ball Chair for the Academy Awards Governors Ball. Sitting in Alan's office, where Marilyn would also join us for tea, I marveled at the Oscars®, Emmys, Golden Globes®, Grammys, gold records, and other awards populating the desk, shelves and walls.

"Alan," I would confess, "I can't believe I'm sitting here with you two. You wrote America's songbook. It's mind-boggling. I'm just stunned."

Alan would reply, "Oh please, Cheryl, forget it. It's no big deal. Are you kidding me?" Marilyn would laugh and agree.

There's never an event of mine that Alan and Marilyn have attended when they haven't sought me out to say hello, and congratulate the team.

I was 16 years old when I first heard and learned to play *The Windmills of Your Mind* on my accordion. I was mesmerized by the music and lyrics. Had I ever heard of Alan Bergman or given much thought to the composer? No, but I remember *The Windmills of Your Mind* as one of the most beautiful songs, with beautiful lyrics written by Alan and Marilyn in 1968.

Alan and Marilyn are living examples of how it's not about who we are, but what we give. (More than a few have inspired me, taught me, and touched my heart; and the list goes on and on.)

*   *   *

I called Alan Bergman, and asked, "Alan, who do you have? I need a great up-and-coming star."

He said, "Judith Hill."

If you had the opportunity to watch the 2014 Oscar-winning documentary *20 Feet From Stardom*, then you know Judith Hill. She is one of the many artists who has supported so much talent over the years, and finally broke ground as a solo artist and star in her own right. Judith has performed at two of our events: the 2013 Academy Awards Governors Ball and the 2014 Primetime Emmys Governors Ball. Her talent, beauty, and down-to-earth charm are absolutely contagious. She makes you want to take up singing. Judith was to go on tour with Michael Jackson. Of course, Mr. Jackson knew a star in the making.

ELLE MACPHERSON   Jan 2013.

Dear Cheryl —
        Just a little note to say how much
i enjoyed working with you and your
team for the 5 day Gala event —
Your organisation, care, professionals in
+ expertise was inspiring.

Special thanks to Meghan + Alex for
their help and Many thanks to
you, of course —
                        love, Elle

Curtis Stone's Grilled Vegetable Lasagna

INGREDIENTS

Ricotta and tomato sauce

2 tablespoons olive oil

1 large brown onion, finely chopped

6 garlic cloves, minced (crushed)

5 large sprigs of fresh thyme

2 bay leaves

1 teaspoon dried oregano

½ teaspoon dried chili flakes

2 cups (16 fl oz/500 ml) dry white wine

3 lb 14 oz (1.75 kg) ripe plum tomatoes, sliced

Sea salt

1 cup (8 oz/225 g) full-cream ricotta cheese

½ cup very coarsely chopped fresh basil

Freshly ground black pepper

Grilled vegetables

1 medium eggplant (aubergine) (about
  1 lb 6 oz (625 g), stem end trimmed, sliced lengthwise
  into ¼ in. (5 mm) thick rounds

Sea salt and freshly ground black pepper

3 tablespoons balsamic vinegar

3 tablespoons olive oil

3 zucchini (courgettes), sliced lengthwise into
  ¼ in. (5 mm) thick rounds

2 red bell capsicums (peppers), cored, seeded, and
  quartered

METHOD

To make the ricotta and tomato sauce

1. Heat a large heavy pan over medium heat. Add the olive oil, then add the onions and garlic and fry, stirring occasionally, for about 5 minutes, or until the onions are tender. Add the thyme, bay leaves, oregano, and chili flakes and cook, stirring often, for about 2 minutes, or until fragrant. Add the wine, increase the heat to high, and boil for about 12 minutes, or until reduced by half.

2. Stir in the tomatoes and season with salt. Bring to a simmer, then reduce the heat to medium-low and simmer gently, uncovered, stirring occasionally, for about 50 minutes, or until the tomatoes are very tender and have broken down to form a chunky sauce.

To prepare the vegetables

1. Arrange the eggplant slices on a baking tray and sprinkle with 1 tablespoon salt. Let stand for about 20 minutes, or until the salt begins to draw out moisture from the eggplant.

2. Rinse the eggplant under cold running water, then drain well. Place on a dry baking tray and pat dry with paper towels.

3. In a small bowl, whisk the vinegar and olive oil together and season with salt and pepper. Arrange the zucchini and capsicums on a large rimmed baking tray and brush both sides of the vegetables with balsamic mixture. Brush the remaining balsamic mixture over both sides of the eggplant slices.

4. Transfer the vegetables to the grill, in batches if necessary, and grill until just tender and slightly charred, about 3 minutes per side for the eggplant and zucchini, and about 4 minutes per side for the capsicums. Return the vegetables to the baking trays as they are cooked and let cool. Cut the capsicums quarters in half.

5. When the sauce is cooked, remove the pan from the heat, then remove and discard the bay leaves and thyme stems. Stir in the ricotta cheese. Purée half of the sauce in a blender. Return the puree to the sauce remaining in the pan and stir in the basil. Season the sauce to taste with salt and pepper.

6. Preheat the oven to 350°F/180°C.

Recipe continues on page 219

Assembly

12 dried lasagna sheets (about 12 oz/350 g)

4 cups (1 lb 2 oz/500 g) mozzarella cheese, shredded

SERVES 10

To assemble the lasagna

1. Spread 1 cup of the tomato sauce over the base of a 12 x 9 x 2 in. (32 x 23 x 5 cm) baking dish. Place 4 uncooked lasagna sheets over the sauce, breaking them to fit (don't worry if there's space around the pasta, since they will expand as they cook). Place one-third of the grilled vegetables over the pasta, then spoon 1½ cups of the sauce over the vegetables and sprinkle ⅓ of the mozzarella cheese over the sauce. Repeat layering the noodles, vegetables, sauce, and mozzarella cheese one more time. Top with the remaining 4 noodles, then spread with 1½ cups of the sauce. Arrange the remaining vegetables on top. Spoon the remaining sauce over the vegetables.

2. Cover the baking dish with aluminum foil. Bake for 45 minutes. Remove the foil and sprinkle the remaining mozzarella over the lasagna. Bake, uncovered, for about 30 minutes, or until the cheese has melted and the lasagna is golden brown on top and heated through (if you insert a knife into the center of the lasagna for 10 seconds, it should feel hot after you pull it out). Let the lasagna stand for 15 minutes before serving.

Photo and recipe courtesy of Curtis Stone

How About You?

Do Try This at Home

Yes, you should.

   Let's shift gears for a minute. The unique flavor and grand style of a Hollywood-sized event is completely feasible in your own home. The key is inspiration and ingenuity, not size or expense.

   Though your elegant soiree or casual garden party may appear to your guests as natural and effortless, as if it just sprung from the ether, I'm here to tell you that for a memorable and flawless affair, that is not the case. Wait! Don't go running into the woods. It's all doable and fun. The key is organization and planning, even if your plans are not elaborate. Good organization is much less stressful than "a wing and a prayer".

NUPTIALS

Here's a template for the most comprehensive and personally important event you're ever likely to host: the family wedding. For any less involved or more spontaneous affair, you can begin your planning with this template and remove the items that don't apply. My ulterior motive here is to demonstrate the detail that goes into an event. The more advanced planning and organization you square away, the less drama and fewer snags will haunt you during the big day.

Your heart of hearts

Don't jump the gun. What's important to you? What is the style or personal taste of the bride and groom? Consider what you envision first, before you plan the nitty-gritty. Consider these check points for ideas:

- Where: Current city? Hometown? Destination wedding?
- Indoors? Outdoors? Hall? Backyard? Beach? Synagogue/Church?
- Theme or style: Is it formal? Casual? Traditional? Eclectic?
- When: Afternoon? Evening? Sunrise?
- Guest count: Intimate or large? Or somewhere in between?
- Guest list: Close family? Good friends? Everyone you know?
- Wedding party list: Best man? Maid of honor? Bridesmaids and groomsmen? Speakers? Children attendants?
- Days before: Engagement party? Bachelor/ Bachelorette party?
- Wedding day weekend: Rehearsal dinner? Out of town guest reception? Farewell luncheon/brunch?

Reality
- When is the venue that you have your heart set on available?
- Are the most important people to you available on the weekend you've chosen?
- Is that month a less than ideal time to travel? Is the weather unpredictable that time of year for such an important, outdoor occasion? (If applicable)
- Is your chosen date on or close to a religious or national holiday?
- Finally—how can your imagination best serve your budget? Plan smart and spend less.

The possibilities are endless

How will you "sign your name" to your celebration and make it memorable? There is so much information out there. This is a perfect time to make friends with Google and Pinterest. Your own tastes deserve broad consideration, but your research will springboard your own imagination to new ideas and uncover possibilities "outside the box". Though I love a classic, elegant undercurrent at any wedding, honoring the significance of the affair, my taste could never be described as "traditional". My taste directs me towards the unique and the surprising. Research what is trending in weddings and in other homegrown or even high profile celebrations. What melding of styles might set off your imagination? What new ideas could set your celebration on its ear?

WHAT'S NEW IN WEDDINGS?

Retro-chic

Retro chic is huge right now, begging for playful ingenuity. A wedding motif rife with vintage detailing, whether from the 1950s, '60s, or even '70s, offers endless décor options. Choose colorful and patterned linens for tables and the buffet, rather than the typical white and crème. Let's face it: your guests have attended many weddings, so surprise them. Gravitate towards the unexpected. Serve your hors d'oeuvres in unique containers, such as stemmed champagne glasses. A mini cup of soup offered along with a bite-size grilled cheese sandwich is a unique, comfort-food crowd pleaser. Dress your guest seating with eyelet runners, and ask your florist to arrange your centerpieces in small porcelain vases, silver pitchers, or copper pots. Rather than the traditional, tiered wedding cake, consider multiple cakes in an eclectic display, or one each displayed on every guest table, or mini cakes of many varieties served to each guest. How about a tiered "cheese" cake, each tier consisting of a fine selection of cheese, garnished with fruit and nuts.

As a general rule, don't forgo the elegance; just include the rustic and unexpected. As an added perk, retro-chic is more economical than traditional china and crystal.

Innovative ceremony setups

In an increasingly casual and connected world, comfort has eclipsed the obligation of rigid tradition. Whether your ceremony takes place in a church, at a farm, or in a ballroom, consider elements that encourage a "right at home" feeling. Skip the expected down-the-middle-aisle scenario, and instead create a living-room vibe with a mix of couches, chairs, and settees. You've already intrigued your guests when you suggested "cocktail casual" in the invitation. Guests are immediately invigorated once they walk into a reimagined ceremony space. Though rented furniture comes at a price, an off-premise event in a rustic location sidesteps what often turns out to be a hefty ballroom bill. Shake it up. Would you consider replacing all those identical, rented wooden chairs with wooden benches covered with quilts? Spread blankets on the ground right in front of the ceremony for the kids. You are only limited by your imagination.

Family style receptions

I always promote choices that encourage mingling and connection as much as possible. Somewhere between stuffy French table service and cafeteria style buffets is the family style sit-down dinner. Think of it as a re-creation of a casual dinner party in your own home. A variety of food and a comfortable setting are both key. Smaller starter plates and a first course of bite-sized options placed at the center of the table stimulate the taste buds and kick start the conversation, because the items are passed guest to guest. You may consider long rectangular tables rather than limit your guests' dinner companions at a round table. For the main course, how about heading back to basics? I've noticed that at bar mitzvahs, many of the adult guests decline the plated dinner and seek out the chicken sliders on the kids' buffet. Perhaps a dinner of family favorites, normally served at your own kitchen table, might be in order? The key is variety. Continuing this theme with the main course, set platters of all the options right on the guest tables and within reach, as well as wine, punch, or lemonade. A spread within arm's reach encourages guests to help themselves, just like they'd do at their own homes. The ice is broken, encouraging conversation and a more intimate atmosphere.

Textured flower arrangements

Tall centerpieces, overflowing with roses and calla lilies, have given way to low, or textural arrangements that recall a springtime garden to mind will act as the focus for any table. Depending on the season, include green moss, crisp autumn foliage, or an evergreen. Line your flower-filled vases with birch-bark leaves. Throw extra color and texture into the mix by wrapping your bouquets in lace or patterned fabric. Request your florist to incorporate small planters, classic pedestals, vintage-inspired vases, and even rustic apple crates.

Entertainment

Everyone loves a live band, though DJs are resurging in popularity. I don't mean the old iPod-and-speakers setup. Skilled, turntable DJs amaze me with their instinctive connection to the vibe, while also leading to its necessary crescendos or mellow interludes. They store a tremendous variety of favorites and refreshing remixes, tailored expertly to your guests' tastes and demographic, guaranteeing a packed, joyous dance floor the whole night. If it's in your budget, hire a specialty band that speaks to your relationship or wedding locale (a jazz trio, bluegrass band, a funk group, or steel drums) for the cocktail hour.

Souped-up photo booths

Entertainment, design ideas, and new technology pop up every day, and a key job of mine is to stay in step with new developments. There's a wonderful, new, photo-booth variation called "Phhhoto". The set-up creates mini, stop-gap movies of several, quick-captured still photos, and sends it immediately to your smart phone to enjoy and share with friends.

Themed engagement photo shoots

Similar to your dress and reception décor, your engagement photo shoot should be completely "you". Following that line of thought, fun-loving couples are coming up with the most creative, themed engagement photo shoots, from *Mad Men* and *Breakfast at Tiffany's* to the 1950s backyard barbecue. Not into the full-on theme idea? Tone it down, providing just props, such as colorful balloons, umbrellas, or a tandem bicycle. You'll notice that, with a little creativity on the front end, your resulting wedding album will contain some of the widest smiles you've ever seen.

Grand exits

We all know about the "grand entrance" to the first dance. What if you brought back the "grand exit", even if it's only to the after party? Besides, your older guests may decide to call it a night at that point. The grand exit makes for great pictures, ending that portion of the evening with fun and togetherness. Alternatives to birdseed: paper airplanes, ticker tape, or sparklers.

TIMELINE

Let's say your wedding is the 6th of June, which is a VERY popular month. Here are deadline reminders to put on the calendar.

12 months

- Set a preliminary budget.
- Research and book your location. Include your rehearsal dinner and goodbye breakfast plans. Some locations book two years in advance. Do you need a back-up location due to weather?
- Write your friends on Facebook, Instagram and other social media for suggestions.
- Reserve a block of hotel rooms at a reduced rate.
- Consider creative ways of asking your best man, maid of honor, and the rest of the wedding party to be a part of your wedding—this sets a tone early on.
- Begin shopping for a dress. Try to place your order 10 to 12 months in advance to avoid rush charges.

11 months

- Start a board on Pinterest of all the elements that speak to your style, from the dress, jewelry, wedding party attire, flowers, etc. It's a great visual way to communicate to your vendors the look and feel you are going for.

OPPOSITE PAGE

Outdoor reception
ZenTodd.com

- Order bridesmaid dresses. You usually need six to eight months max to order bridesmaid dresses.
- Check with your employer regarding time off of work.
- Hire your officiant.
- Hire your photographer—good photographers book early.
- Hire a band or DJ. Remember, Facebook is your friend.
- Book a caterer.
- Choose your florist and reserve the date.
- Consider all of the other details for your wedding—specialty linens, furniture rentals, chairs, candles, and so forth. Consider all the special details that reflect your style and place orders.
- Unless Uncle Bob is filming your wedding, research your videographer in advance. They also need to be booked early.
- Check passport expiration dates. It takes a minimum of six weeks to renew a passport.

10 months
- Send "Save the Date" cards or emails.
- Book your honeymoon.
- Hire lighting and sound or an audio/visual (A/V) company if applicable.
- Shop for wedding rings.
- Measure and order tuxedos.

9 months
- Choose and order invitations. Work on stationary early, especially if sending out Save the Dates six to twelve months in advance. It also gives you the advantage to have a very cohesive look across all of your stationary.

8 months
- Hire a calligrapher, if desired.
- Consider a video presentation of the bride and groom.
- Interview makeup and hairdressers—go for a trial and bring your veil and jewelry, if you have it. Make sure you like the way you look plenty of time before the wedding. Decide if you are also going to host makeup and hair for your attendants. If so, work on timing and see how many people you need to have everyone looking gorgeous and on time for photographers.

7 months
- Hire a limo/car service.
- Book wedding night suite. Where are the wedding party and groomsmen dressing day-of wedding?
- Finalize guest count.

- Determine any allergies or special needs with close relatives and friends.

6 months

- Arrange a cake tasting. It's fun and festive too. Remember to bring a bottle of champagne with you.

2 months

- Send invitations—invitations are typically mailed six to eight weeks prior to the wedding.
- Order party favors, if desired.
- It's time for the best man and maid of honor to organize the bachelor party and bachelorette party!
- Delegate remaining rehearsal dinner and farewell brunch details.
- Organize any medical paperwork for honeymoon.
- Schedule makeup and hair appointments.
- Apply for marriage licence.
- Contact any important guests who have no responded.
- Put together song list for band/DJ.
- Compile a list of potential speakers for the heart-to-heart speeches—best man, father of the bride, maid of honor, anyone else?
- Pay all of your deposits.

1 month

- Purchase any gifts required for officiant or participants.
- Consider welcome baskets for hotel rooms.
- Attend final fitting for wedding dress.
- Confirm transportation schedules.
- Distribute schedule and cell phone numbers to all participants. Send out of town guests a separate letter with important details, driving directions, sites to see, hair salon suggestions, and restaurant recommendations.
- Write vows and speeches.
- Pick up wedding rings!
- Make arrangements with the DJ or band for music of choice.
- Provide photographer and videographer with a shot list.
- Arrange dinner guest seating.
- Map out wedding ceremony transactions/details.
- Contact all vendors and participants to confirm arrangements and payment.
- Skincare management for bride—facials, if needed.
- Check the long range weather forecast.

May 31st
- Delegate as much of the day-of tasks as possible.
- Fully educate all participants regarding their responsibilities.
- Pack for your honeymoon.
- Provide final guest count to caterer.
- Pack for your wedding weekend.

June 3rd
- Check the weather again, and adjust arrangements where necessary.
- Organize any gratuities in advance.

June 4th
- Deliver welcome gifts.
- Every personal item should be double checked.

June 5th
- Rehearsal.
- Rehearsal dinner.
- Speeches.
- Video presentation, if desired.
- Rest!

Saturday morning—Wedding Day
- Relax and enjoy your special day, you deserve it!
- Ladies' hair and makeup calls.
- Groomsmen's call time.
- Florist arrival—corsages and boutonnieres.
- Refreshments.
- Photographer/Videographer arrives.
- Installation complete.
- Decor, lighting, and sound installed.

Saturday midday
- Call time for immediate family and wedding party photographs and video.
- Bride and groom photos.
- Entertainment set-up.
- Flowers placed.

- Cue music.
- Guest arrival.
- Guests called to ceremony.

Ceremony
- Processional.
- Officiant.
- Groom and groomsmen.
- Groom's grandparents.
- Groom's parents.
- Bride's grandparents.
- Bride's parents
- Bridesmaids.
- Maid of honor.
- Ring bearer.
- Flower girl.
- Bride and father/escort.

Recessional
- Reverse order—with of course the bride and groom leading the way.

Cocktail Reception:
- After the ceremony, bride and groom enjoy 20 minutes quiet time.
- Photographs.
- Cocktails and hors d'oeurvres.
- Call/invite guests to dinner.

Dinner
- Grand entrance of bride and groom, and wedding party.
- First dance/dance set.
- First course.
- Maid of honor's speech.
- Mother's speech.
- Mother and son dance/dance set.
- Second course.
- Best man's speech.
- Father's speech.

- Father and daughter dance/dance set.
- Dessert.
- Cake cutting.
- Bride and groom speeches.
- Dance set / bouquet and garter toss.
- Last dance.
- After party.

Tips

My team reminded me of a number of ingenious little tips to streamline the organizational process and solve unexpected challenges:

- Keep chalk to cover up unexpected spills on your wedding dress. It's great to have a toiletry basket for the bridesmaids and groomsmen as they dress for the wedding; you won't believe how many forget a razor or a toothbrush. Keep Band-Aids and a sewing kit on hand for the unexpected.
- Pack a production box, including all the basics such as sharpies, tape, table seating cards, pins, and calligraphy pens.
- Know the contingency plan for Mother Nature's unexpected surprises (i.e. wind, rain, temperature).
- Pack flip-flops for the bride and wedding party.
- Don't wait until the final few days to begin your seating chart. You can always add to it and amend it as you go.
- Number your RSVP cards. You'd be surprised how often people forget to write their name (probably because they're so excited!). You easily fill in the blank.
- My advice to you, if you do not wish to hire a full time coordinator, you may wish to hire a coordinator the day-of or week-of the celebration. "You might be wondering if you did the right thing by hiring extra help the day before the wedding, but I guarantee you that the day after you will be thrilled that you did.

A final note

There is no definitive "formula" to produce a wedding, or any other event for that matter. These are only suggested guidelines. The planning of your own celebration will evolve distinctively, reflecting your vision, taste, unique sensibility, and imagination.

Help Yourself

ABBONDANZA—CASUAL ENTERTAINING, ITALIAN STYLE

Walk into my home, and I will feed you. My husband has been known to say, "Cheryl, the mailman can just deliver the mail."

"Really? I think he is quite enjoying his Frappuccino."

Yes, I'm a working girl, too. Sometimes my life gets the better of my schedule and it takes days to catch up. But time flies. Our schedules don't magically clear up by tomorrow, as we may fantasize that they will, so we should avoid the temptation to put life on hold and start our "real" lives later. With a little planning, and enough time purposefully set aside, we don't have to postpone the celebrating until the opportunity has passed.

I've mentioned that I'm a cookbook and magazine fanatic. My friends have branded me "a foodie" and my youngsters have caught on to this. If I leave a food magazine lying around, my son steals my Post-it® notes, places them on the recipes he's excited to try and leaves the magazines open and easy for me to find.

Here are some suggestions to help you confidently entertain at home (just think of me whispering a few hints and suggestions in your ear as you follow the recipes):

HOME ENTERTAINING

Rule # 1: Be prepared
For at-home entertaining—one of my true joys—I store the necessary items such as hard goods and non-perishable foods close at hand for more spontaneous gatherings and less shopping on the day-of.

Rule #2: Don't cram
A trick to reduce your workload is to spread the food and other preparations over two or three days.

Rule #3: Think like a hostess, not a waiter
Rather than assume the role of glorified waitress, ask yourself what you would enjoy if you were the guest? What tastes, sounds, and sights can you think of that will entice your guests immediately, thus leaving the outside world outside? Guests relax as soon as they discover they are in good hands.

Rule #4: Quality ingredients
Home entertaining is all about the food. Guests come for dinner and stay for the company… and for second helpings. The phenomenal spaghetti sauces my father prepared simmered for four or five hours. I don't think

I ever tasted canned soup when I was young. My parents were supporting a large family and did not spend frivolously, but in terms of ingredients, they did not scrimp where it counted.

Rule #5: An unexpected menu

You might expect this Italian girl to include certain staples from the old country on her entertaining menus. You're right. My menu is frequently Italian, but with a twist. I'm influenced by the ingenuity and whimsy of California cuisine, or "food fusion", with attention paid to presentation. It's a plus that so many Italian-inspired menu possibilities fall into the category of comfort food and are, therefore, crowd pleasers.

ABOVE
Family reunion in Sudbury,
Ontario, Canada

Rule #6: Learn from food

Mastering a recipe is a process, as is ultimately relaxing into cooking. Preparing a recipe a number of times will render it second nature and enjoyable. Connoisseurs of fabulous wine master their skills over time through study, learning from the masters, and tasting a great variation of wines. Connoisseurs of food are no different. We must taste again and again to understand ingredients and their flavors. Learn to taste your cooking; it directs you where to take it.

Rule #7: Flexibility

You may, of course, substitute any of these menu suggestions with specialties of your own, or items simpler to prepare, or with fewer choices. Good food is not necessarily derived from a daunting recipe. When choosing your menu, pardon the pun, you need not bite off more than you can chew.

Rule #8: Safety in numbers

Remember my cardinal rule: a compadre in the kitchen adds to the fun, shares the responsibility and eases the pressure. The first line in every recipe should read: "Uncork a bottle of red. Pour two glasses. Sip. Cook. Laugh". The party's already started.

PRESENTATION

I usually opt to serve buffet style, allowing guests to choose according to tastes, appetites and specific dietary needs. Better still, if my guest count is smaller, I serve family style at my dining room table, every platter within reach of either you or your dinner companions.

A feast for the eye, I prefer symmetrical platters and patterns on a buffet, or picture-perfect portions on a plate. Don't overcrowd, however, do garnish generously with aromatic herbs.

The menu
Suggestions:
Italian Cheese Plate (see page 242)
Prosciutto and Figs (see page 241)
Arugula Salad (see page 243)
Cheryl's Cioppino (see page 103)
Polenta (see page 242)
Elsie's Manicotti (see page 240)
Elsie's Italian Stuffed Tomatoes (see page 243)
My Sisters' Blueberry Pie (see page 279)
Chic's Zabaglione (see page 244)

OPPOSITE PAGE
Baked bean cook-off
selections at Cecchetto
family reunion in Sudbury,
Ontario, Canada

Elsie's Manicotti

INGREDIENTS

Marinara sauce

4 x 14 oz (400 g) cans whole tomatoes

¼ cup (2 fl oz/60 ml) extra virgin olive oil

1 small yellow onion, peeled and minced (crushed)

2 cloves garlic, peeled and minced (crushed)

Sea salt

6–10 fresh basil leaves, torn

Pinch of dried oregano

Freshly ground black pepper

Pasta dough

4 sheets pasta dough, each 8½ x 11 in. (20 x 27 cm)

Filling

1 cup (3 oz/85 g) fresh Parmesan, grated

1 cup (8 oz/225 g) whole-milk ricotta cheese

1 cup (7 oz/180 g) steamed and chopped fresh spinach

½ cup (3½ oz/100 g) fresh mozzarella cheese, shredded

METHOD

For the marinara sauce

1. Drain the tomatoes over a bowl, reserving the juice. Crush the tomatoes with your hands into the same bowl, gently removing and discarding any hard cores, skin, or tough membranes from stem ends. Set aside.

2. Heat the olive oil in a large pan over medium-low heat. Add the onions and cook until golden, about 10 minutes. Add the garlic and sauté until soft, about 3 minutes. Stir in the crushed tomatoes and reserved juice and season to taste with salt. Increase the heat to high and bring the sauce to a boil.

3. Immediately reduce the heat to low and simmer until the sauce has thickened slightly, about 1 hour.

4. Stir in the basil and oregano and season to taste with salt and pepper. If not using immediately, set aside to cool, then cover and refrigerate, covered for up to 1 week, or freeze.

For the pasta

1. Cut each pasta sheet into 6 rectangles, about 3 × 4 in. (7.5 x 10 cm).

For the filling

1. Preheat the oven to 350°F/180°C.

2. Combine the filling ingredients in a bowl and mix well. Spread 2 heaping teaspoons of filling on the longest side of each rectangle. Roll up from the long side but do not fold in the ends.

3. Tip ¼ in. (6 mm) of the marinara sauce in the base of 2 baking dishes each 9 × 13 in. (22 x 33 cm).

4. Divide the pasta rolls evenly between each baking dish. Top with the remaining marinara sauce, dividing evenly.

5. Bake for 45 minutes or until the pasta is cooked through.

6. Top with additional Parmesan and shredded mozzarella just before serving. Run under broiler for a minute, if desired.

Pasta Dough

INGREDIENTS

3½–4 cups (14–16 oz/400–450 g) all-purpose (plain) flour, sifted, plus extra for dusting

4 large eggs

½ teaspoon extra-virgin olive oil

METHOD

1. Mound the flour on a clean work surface. Make a well in the center.
2. In a bowl, whisk the eggs and oil together to combine. Gently pour in the eggs mixture into the well. Beat, incorporating the flour closest to the liquid in order to avoid a spill.
3. Once the dough begins to hold together, switch from the fork to kneading the dough with your hands. Lift the dough off the work surface, dust the surface with flour, and continue kneading until the dough is completely mixed together and fluffy. Don't worry if it's a little sticky. That's a good thing.
4. Wrap the dough in plastic wrap (cling film) and set aside for 30 minutes.
5. Your dough is ready to be formed into manicotti shells (see manicotti recipe).

◦ ◦ ◦

Prosciutto and Figs

INGREDIENTS

12 oz (340 g) prosciutto, thinly sliced (trim off any fat)

8 fresh figs

Fresh basil leaves

Freshly ground pepper

2 limes

Parmesan crisps or herb-crusted breadsticks, to serve

Pinot Grigio, to serve

METHOD

1. Arrange the prosciutto loosely or in rolls on a large platter.
2. Cut the figs into wedges or halves and fan in toward the center.
3. Clean the basil leaves and arrange on one side of plate (or in a small bowl on plate). Sprinkle the platter with freshly ground pepper.
4. Refrigerate, covered, until ready to serve. Just before serving, cut the limes into thin wedges. Using one or two lime wedges, squeeze a little lime juice on prosciutto. Arrange the rest of the wedges around the platter.
5. Serve with Parmesan crisps or herb-crusted breadsticks and a glass of Pinot Grigio wine, if desired.

Polenta

INGREDIENTS

7 cups (3 pints/1.6 litres) cold water

1 tablespoon sea salt

2 bay leaves

1 ⅔ cups (6½ oz/185 g) fine yellow or white cornmeal
(polenta)

2 tablespoons butter

Salt and freshly ground black pepper

Parmesan, grated (shredded)

METHOD

1. Pour the cold water, salt and bay leaves into a heavy pan.
2. Stir in the cornmeal (adding cornmeal to cold water helps keep polenta free of lumps). Bring to a boil over high heat, then add the butter.
3. Reduce the heat to medium-low and continue cooking, stirring often with a wooden spoon, until the polenta thickens and pulls away from the base and sides of the pan (about 30–40 minutes).
4. Season to taste with salt and pepper. Discard the bay leaves. Top with Parmesan. Serve hot.

○ ○ ○

Italian Cheese Plate

INGREDIENTS

8 oz (225 g) Gorgonzola

8 oz (225 g) Taleggio

8 oz (225 g) La Tur

8 oz (225 g) Sottocenere with truffle

Assorted Italian olives

Fresh baguette slices and crackers

METHOD

1. Arrange the Italian cheeses on a plate (and attach handwritten identification labels to each). Place a small dish of olives in the center.
2. Serve with baguette slices and crackers.

Elsie's Stuffed Tomatoes

INGREDIENTS

6 large beefsteak tomatoes, halved

2 cups (8 oz/225 g) breadcrumbs

6 tablespoons grated (shredded) Parmesan

1 tablespoon garlic, crushed

6 tablespoons chopped fresh parsley

Salt and pepper, to taste

¼ cup (2 fl oz/60 ml) olive oil

1 oz (30 g) butter

METHOD

1. Preheat oven to 325°F/160°C.
2. Slice the top off each tomato, then slice each top in half. Cut a sliver off the base of each tomato so that they will stand up.
3. Remove the tomato pulp to a bowl. Add the breadcrumbs, cheese, garlic, parsley and salt and pepper, to taste. Mix well.
4. Add just enough of the olive oil until the mixture starts to hold together—it should not be wet.
5. Fill each tomato shell with breadcrumb mixture. Dab the top with butter.
6. Bake for 30–40 minutes, or until the tops are golden brown. Serve immediately.

○ ○ ○

Arugula Salad

INGREDIENTS

4 x 5–7 oz (150–210g) bags pre-washed arugula (rocket)

¾ cup (6 fl oz/175 ml) extra virgin olive oil

Sea salt, to taste

¼ cup (2 fl oz/60 ml) balsamic vinegar

Freshly cracked pepper, to taste

1 lb (450 g) teardrop (cherry) tomatoes

3 avocados, cut into ¼ in. (6 mm) wedges

Parmesan, shaved

METHOD

1. In a bowl, mix the arugula with the oil and salt, then toss with balsamic vinegar and pepper.
2. Arrange the tomatoes in the center and fan the avocado wedges around them.
3. Scatter with shaved Parmesan.

Chic's Zabaglione

INGREDIENTS

4 egg yolks

¼ cup (2 oz/60 g) sugar

½ cup (4 fl oz/125 ml) marsala

Whipped cream, chocolate shavings and berries, to serve

METHOD

1. Combine the egg yolks and sugar into a large stainless-steel mixing bowl. Whisk until thin and pale yellow, about 5 minutes.

2. Simmer (not boil) yolk and sugar mixture in double broiler.

3. Gradually drizzle in the marsala, while whisking continuously until the mixture is light and foamy, almost triples in volume, about 15 minutes. Do not let the egg cook around the edges of the bowl.

4. Spoon into 4 small dessert dishes (or stemmed glasses) and serve either warm, at room temperature, or chilled, topped with whipped cream, chocolate shavings, and cranberries or strawberries.

The Envelope Please

AWARDS NIGHT PARTY

How about a Hollywood-style party of your own? The focus is on the fun, rather than the pomp and circumstance.

With a little ingenuity, and the readily available reference points that are out there, the red carpet on Hollywood Boulevard is as close as the end of your own driveway.

A large proportion of the events we produce, and those most televised, are awards shows. Awards season generally falls between January and March, and celebrates the artistic achievements of the previous year. The two exceptions are the Tony Awards® in June, and the Emmys® in August or September. Maybe it's a time of year when your friends and neighbors are at home and might appreciate a little merriment?

The installation of the Governors Ball begins a full two weeks before the orchestra hits the downbeat. Pre-production commences many months before that. My point is that you must also plan ahead for success. Your early planning includes the following:

- Save the Date: Of course, you must host your awards party on the same night as Hollywood. Send your guests a Save the Date email or invite as soon as you decide to take the plunge because Hollywood's date is firm. The design of your Save the Date invitations already sets the tone for a creative, exciting night and ensures the largest number of "yes" responses. You may have a son, daughter, or close friend who is a whiz at the computer to assist with your design. Your invitation indicates that this will not be a late-night party, as the telecast will likely end by 11:00 p.m. depending on your time zone.

- Check in with your closest friends and family for helpers. You don't need to go it alone. They will have fun as your assistants, with inspiration of their own!

Okay, you've taken care of your preliminary deadlines and commitments. Now, back to your party planning.

A little ingenuity via creative invitations, themed décor, entertainment, and unique food choices will tantalize your guests to arrive, enjoy and stay. Here are 10 Hollywood Awards Party Must-Haves to set your celebration up for success!

1. My priority is always to connect my guests in some way. Encourage your guests to watch as many of the nominated films or television shows as possible, or listen to nominated music on YouTube. When they "do their homework", lively debate and predictions over who deserves to take home the gold will abound.

2. Set your arrival time at one hour before the awards show begins. There's plenty of games, food, cocktails, and of course, socializing to cover! Plan to offer some substantial fare, as they will assume your soirée covers the dinner hour. Invite your guests early to enjoy the pre-show red carpet arrivals and vote for best

dressed. Also create a ballot to cast predictions for the evening's winners and give fun prizes relating to the theme.

3. If your party is formal, suggest that your guests wear black and white. A hint of collective "costuming" is social and fun.

4. Play the soundtracks of nominated films or music as your guests arrive.

5. Awards season calls for champagne, champagne and more champagne! A splash of bubbly encourages celebration and mingling and is a necessity in order to toast the winners. For a fizzy, non-alcoholic alternative, mix pomegranate juice and soda water, then garnish with a mint sprig.

6. Theme everything. How about a few apropos names for your signature cocktails? A few of my favorites are: "And The Cosmo Goes To", "Mixologist and Mingle" and for your pomegranate offering, what else but "The Red Carpet".

7. The Ballot Game. Download and print the nominations in the various categories. Guests will fill them out before the show begins, or if you sent them with the invitation, at home before they arrive. Keep score during the show. Which of your guests are ahead, and who's clearly been a shut-in for the last twelve months? The three guests with the most correct answers at the end of the show win! Choose prizes that are an extension of that awards show. Your shut-in gets a booby prize!

8. A sit-down dinner is not necessarily conducive to a party centered around the screen. Rather than a large entrée, serve an accumulating assortment of delicious, small bites throughout the evening. Place within reach and they'll disappear on their own. Introducing appetizers as your night progresses will both delight and intrigue your guests. Surprises are a key component of good entertaining. Guests who don't know what's around the corner are happier and stick around. Eclectic, slightly unusual food offerings are best, but definitely include one or two for which you are locally famous. Perhaps you'll ask some of your friends to prepare a few appetizers of their own, and share the limelight.

9. It's amazing how the little details are what people remember. A casual but elegant atmosphere invariably calls for flowers and candles. Nature adds life and charm to any indoor setting. At your local flower mart, challenge yourself to choose blooms you've never considered before, and fashion the arrangements yourself, with your own personal touches. Most awards are gold, therefore, add gold touches with ribbons around your candles, faux gold chargers to pass hors d'oeuvres, and perhaps incorporate gold into your outfit!

10. If your heart is set on a sit-down dinner—absolutely! Accent with tabletop glitz and glamour. Head over to your local fabric store and pick a few fabrics that sparkle, adding them as a tablecloth or accent. The glassware, china or cutlery you place will look fabulous against your sparkling choices.

11. Who doesn't like party favors? Offer your guests a fun parting gift, themed for the evening.

Know Thyself

REALITY CHECK FOR ASPIRING PARTY PLANNERS

One of my goals in writing this book is to create a beautiful and stimulating conversation starter for your coffee table. Though not a "how to do it yourself" book, I'd love to hear that this book did, in fact, initiate some Hollywood-inspired, homegrown entertaining. So many people whose paths I cross ask me, "So how did you get here?" Well, funny they should ask, and now they know. Be honest, did you pick up this book because you are entertaining the notion of doing this for a living?

Is this for you?

It's true; the special event industry carries with it a glamorous appeal. The stunning designs, the fancy people—all can certainly be captivating. What follows is a bit of a reality check, my gift to you, should you be considering special events as a career.

Talent

You hopefully possess a natural ability and a passion for your chosen career. Sometimes, passion leads and the not-so-natural talent is learned over time. The good news is: someone who loves something is often also very good at it from the get-go. Natural talent is no excuse for anyone to feel entitled or to expect opportunities to come straight to them just because they think they are deserving. If they "just had the chance" or "just knew the right people", everything would magically occur. No. Let's take our cue from Charlie Brown who, after losing yet another baseball game, lamented, "How can we lose when we are so sincere?" Sorry, Charlie, you can't win just by wanting or wishing, or by just being a good person.

Intention

I think it's helpful to write your passion on paper, long hand. This is your mission statement, if you will. Write it, cross things out, add something else and tweak it until it's just right. Quite a while ago, after several attempts, I came up with my own: "Envision and manifest unique, transcending events that celebrate, honor, and reconnect human relationships."

Work ethic

How will you put your mission statement into effect? If your (1) talent for creativity in entertaining, and (2) passion to do it does not manifest into (3) a no-nonsense, no-fooling, get-serious work ethic, then you should run, screaming, in the opposite direction. We know that the same roll-up-your-sleeves rule goes for medical students, dancers, stockbrokers, painters, and pretty much everybody else. The crucially important habit that we must cultivate, the one that Charlie Brown neglected, is hard work, practice and not expecting overnight success. I don't care how much we might meditate or chant or be kind to animals (well, please be kind to animals), but it's not good enough just to love something, or even have a talent for it. My dear friend Shelley Winters put it this way, "Find out what you are good at, and do that like gangbusters."

Shelley hit the nail on the head. Essentially, she was talking about work ethic. Don't live in fantasy and believe that your chosen field is easy. If it was easy, a lot of unmotivated people would excel at it.

Our passion for our chosen field is what fuels our consistent hard work, beyond when we are tired and beyond when we would prefer to call it a day. It drives us through sacrifice and delayed gratification, toward our goals. Our work day must be one of meaning and purpose, rather than drudgery. Please don't resonate with those fortunate few whose joy in life seems to have fallen into their laps. Was it Lana Turner, the famous movie actress of the '40s, who was supposedly "discovered" sipping coffee at a drugstore counter? Well, that's great for her. We hear about people who are overnight successes all the time, when that's not actually the case. For those who are, I'm happy for them, but they are in a tiny minority.

Education

In most fields, even if your intent is to launch a business of your own, the rule of thumb is to first work for a company in that field, spending three years learning everything that you can. You'll begin, very possibly, at an entry-level position. Work diligently, make yourself indispensable, learn the ropes, develop expertise, and over time, move up through the ranks. There is a large vocabulary of skills to master.

Your natural role

If the prospect of working in special events really appeals to you, but the self-drive to tenaciously build your own business via relentless blood, sweat, and tears feels daunting, then consider working as an employee for a company where your responsibilities and structure are laid out for you. An employee is more often in a position to leave the office behind at 5:30 p.m., be home most nights for dinner, and even have most weekends free. You may not need to be concerned with your inbox until 8:30 a.m. on Monday. There's something to be said for that, as well as a regular paycheck and benefits. Many people prefer the security and structure of such a position. Employers, on the other hand, carry the responsibility of the success of the entire company squarely on their shoulders, as well as the welfare of all of their employees.

On your own

Once you have the knowledge and experience and you feel you are ready, the time may be right to launch out on your own. I recommend that you start small. I started my company on my dining room table, eventually hiring one assistant, then carpeting my garage for my first office, and so on. As a fledgling company, until you've arrived at a level of success where you can hire staff and delegate, you must be proficient at everything. For a time, consider yourself not as small-time, but as a "boutique" event company.

Partnership

Eventually, or even initially, consider a co-owner, or hiring a V.P. who will share much of the responsibility, combined goals, challenges and successes. Just as medical students find study partners and gym partners schedule time to work out together, business people also benefit from the camaraderie, mutual motivation and reality checks of trusted partnerships. Your choice of partner, should you go that route, will be one of the most important decisions of your life. Think of it as a marriage. You should know, in your heart of hearts, whether or not you have the personality to trust and work shoulder-to-shoulder with a partner. Partnership is not for everyone.

Leadership

To meet what I hope will be your own very high standards, you must train your whole team, encourage them, partner with them, demand excellence, and nourish them both individually and as a cohesive group. I'm talking about those you employ—your entire production team—including specialists who provide many of the specific elements of your events, such as flowers, linens, rigging, lighting, music, and so on.

Assertion

You will experience competition, resistance from the occasional vendor who doesn't want to deliver, clients who are reticent to think outside the box, employees who don't cut it, and you will receive checks that sometimes bounce. A fair and compassionate leader is also the person who dismisses the incompetent employee. It comes with the territory. Though sometimes what's required of a leader is offering a cup of tea and an understanding ear.

People person

As an event producer you will wear many hats, and you must wear them all well. You are, all at once: vendor, client, visionary, pragmatist, people-person, teacher, student, foreman, confidante, cheerleader, and especially, assertive taskmaster. An event producer must collaborate with many different personalities, respect them and even enjoy them. Your world includes numbers people, creative people, designers, artisans, technicians, leaders, worker-bees, and your vital, first-contact person; the one who answers the phone and is an ambassador for your company. In the special event world, as with any creative field, you will also discover that many players who live in their "right brains" can be inventive, inspired, even ingenious, and frankly, nuts. You'll quickly know who may require a little organizational assistance. Never write anyone off. Their ideas are often fantastic.

Gratitude

Give credit where credit is due. Your production team's success is your success. They are the wind beneath your wings. I've worked with some of my team for 25 years. Keep your friends close and your colleagues closer! Many of them will be one and the same.

It bears repeating that to be very successful in any business, you must possess the instinct to be your own boss, a passion and ability to excel at your particular talent and the work ethic to see it through.

OPPOSITE PAGE
Fitted in fabulous gowns
for over a decade by
renowned dress designer
Ali Rahimi, and John Barle
of Mon Atelier

Staying Power

If your calling truly is special event production and you're ready to fully commit, then here are twenty clear guidelines for longevity in the business:

1. Purpose

During the conception and execution of a project, look for meaning. Why are we doing this? What's the larger purpose of this project and the reason that it exists? What relationships can be forged, what boundaries expanded, what revelation experienced? How can we apply and expand our own values in this endeavor?

2. Structure

Write lists and make plans. A written plan with a timetable to accomplish it is not limiting. Instead it frees me because I can relax (more or less), knowing that all the bases are covered. With a clear list, I can do one thing at a time. Structure allows me to welcome spontaneity. Write out a schedule and, voilà, you've found more time than you realized. Remember to factor in a contingency plan in your schedule for the unexpected. Your plan may evolve and change and that's okay. Does your schedule ever crash and burn? Of course: it's progress you are after, not perfection.

3. Action and persistence

Work ethic is everything. When in doubt, just begin. When discouraged, persist. Don't wait until you feel like it or until you've figured everything out. Create your own light at the end of the tunnel. Take the plunge. Once you start, it's not as mind-boggling as you thought it was going to be. Fresh ideas and possibilities visit you as soon as you get started.

4. Positivity

Positivity is a perspective you choose so that negativity doesn't choose you. There's never a problem, only a challenge and a solution. Lemons provide the opportunity to make lemonade.

I remember a chef at one of my events ran out of one of the dessert choices. Rather than tell one of the guests that they could not have their choice, he marched into the ballroom and right up to his favorite celebrity, Cybill Shepherd. "Miss Shepherd," he said, "I'm your biggest fan, and it would be an honor if I could prepare a special dessert just for you." Cybill was completely charmed. The challenge of a food shortage was transformed into an opportunity to excel.

5. Empower your team

Hire people who are smarter than you. A great employee or vendor is one whose work ethic and passion for success is as strong as yours. Understand each staff member's strengths and cast them in the particular role that fits them.

6. Take risks

Develop fresh, bold ideas. In Los Angeles, clients and guests usually attend many functions, and they may think they have seen it all. It's our job to surprise them.

7. Know your client

Discover and understand your client's taste and style. Don't rush into production. Interpret and clearly grasp what the mission statement is for the event, then collaborate so you embark in the right direction.

8. Service

A commitment to precise service motivates our every decision on a project. Whether correcting the focus of a single flower arrangement pinspot, or memorizing a VIP's favorite beverage before he or she arrives,

ABOVE
With Gary, Peri and Sequoia
Productions' team
Jerick Dizon

we never leave anything just "good enough". Focusing on service in all of your decisions will steer you in the right direction. Detailed service puts your guests at ease so that they are free to enjoy themselves and experience what you have created. Your commitment to service strengthens your relationship with your client and their trust in you.

9. Communicate

Listen. If we have the strength to speak, we should have the courage to listen, otherwise we might miss out on a very good idea. In order for everyone to be on the same page, voice how you feel and invite others to do the same. Seek a common goal.

10. Compromise

We've worked with very talented clients, including committees. Embrace their input and ideas. Learn from them. With multiple clients, you need to be a person who can manage creative personalities.

11. Create a transcendent experience

I'm very interested in transporting guests via all of the senses. It may be a wonderful wine that highlights one guest's experience or a riveting performer who enchants another. If your guests depart in an elevated state, you've done your job.

12. Streamlining

Ensure that your client and guest experience is easy and seamless. Leave nothing to chance. Incorporate foot traffic controllers, hosts, reserved areas, directional signage, and any opportunity to provide guests with all the information and guidance possible in order to ensure that they have an effortless experience.

13. Build your body of work

Grow. Gain experience wherever you are. Visit trade shows and museums, and attend other events. Discover everything new and exciting emerging from the world of design and entertainment. Take nothing for granted. I truly believe that my work is only as good as my last event.

14. Do what you hate before noon

If there's a job at hand that I loath to begin, invariably that is the job that most needs my attention right away. Transform your weakness into one of your greatest strengths by working at it. Handle what you're avoiding early, and by noon you can have some fun with the elements you love.

15. Avoid immediate gratification

We've all heard the saying "A job worth doing is worth doing well". It's supposed to be hard, or it wouldn't be worthwhile. Accomplish manageable tasks, one at a time, rather than be paralyzed because the job appears too big to tackle. That's where your list comes in.

16. Honesty

Admit when you need help. Come to an agreement. Say "Let's try this," not "You do this" or "Help me out with this" instead of "Stop it". Full communication is more efficient and less stressful. Tell the truth when you make a mistake: perhaps an event gaffe wasn't technically your fault, but it happened, so own up to it with the client. The title "producer" equals "responsibility."

17. Generosity

In our work it's ideally about what we give, not what we get. The bigger picture is: What do we have to contribute? How might we make a difference? How do we wish to be remembered? Scratch that. How do we hope our contribution is remembered? How can we know, in our twilight years, that we "did good"?

18. Gratitude

Appreciate those around you, often and loudly. They contribute so much to your success and your fulfillment in life. Send thank you notes and flowers. Stand up at the dinner table and toast. People work for gratitude and validation as much as they do for money. They care. Cherish them.

19. Be a visionary

My ideas can be so outrageous, I need a team and vendors who are willing to say, "Okay, Cheryl, this one's really crazy, but let's give it a shot." The existence of "the box" presents us with the challenge to live outside of it…

20. Fun

Find the fun and spread it around!

Richard Mooney's Sea Bass Primavera with Salsa Verde

INGREDIENTS

Sea Bass Primavera

4 sea bass fillets, each 6 oz (170 g), skin on

Freshly ground black pepper and sea salt

1 shallot, peeled and thinly sliced

Grated zest of ½ lemon

Few sprigs of fresh dill, coarsely chopped

Drizzle of extra virgin olive oil

20 tender asparagus spears, trimmed of woody ends

8 young carrots, peeled and cut into attractive pieces

Butter

Salsa Verde

1 bunch of Italian parsley, leaves only

1 bunch of mint, leaves only

1 bunch of dill, leaves only

A few celery leaves

2 tablespoons capers, rinsed and dried

¼ teaspoon red chili flakes, or to taste

½–1 cup (4–8 fl oz/125–250 ml) extra virgin olive oil

SERVES 4

METHOD

For the salsa verde

1. Place the parsley, mint, dill, celery leaves, capers and chili flakes in the blender. Add a drizzle of oil and blend to a smooth purée, then add enough oil to make a light pouring consistency. Taste and season with salt and pepper.

For the sea bass primavera

1. Place the fish fillets on a plate and season with a few turns of ground pepper and pinch of sea salt.
2. In a small bowl, mix together the shallot, lemon zest, dill, and extra virgin olive oil. Use to coat the fish, then set aside for 1 hour or overnight.
3. Meanwhile, prepare the vegetables. Blanch the vegetables separately and in batches by dropping stems of asparagus and carrots into salted boiling water. Cook until al dente then remove with a slotted spoon and plunge into an ice bath to arrest the cooking and set the color. Wrap in a kitchen towel and set aside.
4. Preheat the oven to 350°F/180°C. Heat a heavy ovenproof skillet over high heat. Remove the fish from the marinade and place skin side down in the skillet for a few minutes to crisp and char the skin.
5. Place the skillet in the oven for approximately 10 minutes. Do not overcook, check the fish after 7–8 minutes, remembering that it will continue to cook once removed from the oven.
6. While the fish is in the oven, cook the carrots and asparagus in some butter with a little salt and cracked black pepper.
7. Arrange the fish, skin side up on four plates. Surround with the asparagus and carrots and a generous dollop of the salsa verde.

Recipe courtesy of Michael Sullivan

CHAPTER 9

What's It All About?

Life is Short–You Don't Want to Miss It

R & R

I work hard and I do it now, not later. In the same breath, I can tell you that I don't live to work.

I can't always control my time. In fact, there are times when life throws me so many curves that I'm not sure that I'm keeping up, and I can't seem to get out from under. But it's important that I remember the big picture.

Tomorrow never comes and what's past is past. The big picture is today.

In the blink of an eye, my children are already in high school. The AARP (American Association of Retired Persons) mailings appear in my box almost daily. They are really early, thank you very much, but the day is coming. Just like my father said, "Life goes by like that."

We often think to ourselves, "There isn't enough time in the day." If we were given an eighth day of the week, how would we spend that time? Would we take our dogs to the park or read a few more chapters of that dusty book on the night table? Would we go to the gym? The fact is, these are the opportunities, the "quality of life" details that we need to fit into the actual seven days we are allotted because the following seven days will be just as busy and another week of our lives will have gone by.

I've learned to break out my mom's china and pull the good glasses down from the top shelf, even if it's Tuesday.

Do it now. Life is short. These are the good old days, and we don't want to miss them.

PAGE 260

With sisters Carol Quantz,
(left) and Celia Fotes (right)
at the 85th Academy Awards®
Governors Ball
©A.M.P.A.S.
Oscar Statuette ©A.M.P.A.S.®

OPPOSITE PAGE
Top: Cecchetto sisters
Bottom left: With Sequoia
Productions wannabe
Canadians in Sudbury,
Ontario, Canada
Bottom right:
Sequoia Productions
holiday party
Jerick Dizon

I Can't, I'm On the Phone

TECHNOLOGY

Several years ago, a dear family friend was walking to an ice skating party with my son, Milan, 10 years old at the time, and six of his friends. They were walking down a city street, festive with Christmas decorations and music in 70 degree heat in sunny Santa Monica, California. Yet the boys' heads were buried into their phones, texting. Finally, one of the boys walked right into a parking meter. Milan's chums all laughed, as did he, but my friend asked them, "Boys, will you look at what you're doing? No matter whom you're with, you seem to want to be 'talking' with somebody else! We are here, together, so put the phones away!"

The other parents and chaperones agreed immediately, and a few put away their own phones, as well.

The cliché "fast-paced world" is truer these days than ever before. We've bought into this instant, supposed connectivity via email, texting, Instagram, FaceTime —I'm missing a few, probably. What do I know? I think that I was the last person on my block to get a cell phone, and then the last to be brought online, kicking and screaming. Now I field more than 400 emails a day. This is progress? Electronic interfacing may well be a necessary evil in an increasingly scheduled world. Whoever imagined that our children's timetables would become more cluttered than our own?

In terms of our everyday, human lives, this preoccupation with cyber communication eclipses our visceral connection. It renders us with our heads literally in the "cloud", rather than down here in our bodies and souls and with each other. How often, when we type LOL, are we really laughing? "Oh, this is where I'd be laughing if we were actually talking to each other the old-fashioned way." What's next? Will "X" replace kissing and "O" replace hugging?

In my day, our household had one phone. It was a dial phone, an obnoxious bright green one. You know, the one with the curly cord, fixed to the kitchen wall? Granted, my father installed a ridiculously long curly cord, so that we girls could gab with friends in various spots around the house in relative privacy. You could find who was hogging the phone by following the cord. When we left the house, the phone was left behind, without an answering machine. Whoever may have called would call back, unless we ran into them first. Any communication was an actual conversation, not through a screen or keyboard. I remember the time when electronic communication amounted to one rotary phone to every household.

What is this new propensity to communicate once-removed? Sometimes it's immediate, but not always. Much of electronic communicating comes with an additionally insular "hold" button. It's much easier to deflect or ignore someone's email, text, or tweet, than if they were tapping us on the shoulder. Whether immediate or not, it's also at a safe distance. Safe from what? I don't want "my people to call your people". I want to see you, in the flesh. I want to hug. Talk. Laugh.

Time flies so hang up your (not so) smartphone! Your life is calling.

OPPOSITE PAGE

Sequoia Productions
team dials in

Paying it Forward

DOING SOME GOOD

In the midst of an economic downturn, the question is sometimes posed, "How can we throw lavish events when so many people are feeling the effects of austerity?" Throughout the year, and especially during "awards season", the propensity of the Hollywood entertainment industry to celebrate provides employment to thousands of local individuals, as well as to the various media outlets all over the world. Vendors, union personnel, day laborers and other workers would lose a significant portion of their annual income if many events were to be cancelled. Employed people support, as a ripple effect, community businesses, restaurants, etc.

We are fortunate for the opportunity to employ and be employed by an industry that supports so many skilled craftsmen, artisans and technicians. In 2009 and 2010, providing jobs and moving money were essential to bridge the temporary financial challenges of the recession, and support the economic recovery. I enjoyed the sight of hundreds of happily employed waiters facing the front doors, anticipating guest arrival, when so many others were experiencing difficulty finding employment. I hope we assisted in keeping the planet turning.

I'm certain most people work for not only a paycheck, but also for a sense of purpose—for making a valuable difference. Following our larger productions, we endeavor to donate food overages to organizations such as the Los Angeles Mission. Our design materials are sometimes repurposed, and always recycled when appropriate. As our clients and business associates have experienced, we prefer to offer non-traditional holiday gifts, such as supporting national or international charities, or donating to schools whose funding has been drastically cut. During the holidays, the Sequoia team sponsors individual families who appreciate extra support with essentials that many of us take for granted.

My family supports two children in Chiapas, Mexico, the same age as my own children, whom we recently were able to visit. Mia and Milan have corresponded with their "foster friends" for almost all of their lives. It is important to me that my children see for themselves, first hand, a human experience very different from their own. We were so honored to share a face-to-face connection with the children and their families, communicating as best we could through their interpreter, bridging the language and cultural divide. The idea of the trip was initiated by my daughter Mia. Locally, we purchased much needed basic supplies for their school. The entire experience was truly, deeply rewarding.

I recently traveled to the Philippines for a speaking engagement, allowing me the opportunity to interact and share experiences with some truly wonderful, open-hearted people. I was in my hotel room one morning ordering room service—grateful for the warmth and enthusiastic hospitality that the Filipino people are known for—when I noticed outside my hotel window, was an area of the city where people lived literally in

shacks, one on top of the other. My assistant, Chelsea, and I realized that we could not leave the country without figuring out how to make a difference. After a few inquiries, it was suggested we contact House of Hope, an organization that houses entire families, while their children are treated for stage 3–5 cancer. We found ourselves piling up carts of non-perishable foods (as House of Hope does not have refrigeration) and modest toys for the children from local shops. Due to the exchange rate, our dollars went very far. Chelsea and I experienced an excitement of being able to help in some small way. It was humbling and joyful.

Isn't it interesting how, when we travel the world, connecting with unique cultures with vastly different circumstances, we learn more about ourselves and discover opportunities to make a difference. It is said in the Philippines that possession of a running automobile places you within one percent of the wealthiest people in the country. Whenever I'm lamenting about the inconvenience of being stuck in rush-hour traffic, that fact offers a plain and simple reality check. We are, all of us, honored with the opportunity to share our blessings whenever and however we can.

ABOVE
Cecchetto-Michaud family
visits foster family in
Chiapas, Mexico

PAGE 268
Cecchetto-Michaud family
tours Chiapas, Mexico with
their foster family

PAGE 269
Visiting House of Hope
cancer patients and
their families in Davao,
Philippines

Community

PASSING JUDGMENT

In December 2013, I was honored to serve as one of the three judges at the 2014 annual Tournament of Roses® Parade in Pasadena, California. The Committee felt that my experience in special event entertainment and design-centered production would lend itself to the huge responsibility of judging the spectacular parade floats. I jumped at the chance to participate in such an auspicious and community-driven endeavor. The 2014 Rose Parade was particularly significant as it marked the event's 125th anniversary. I was also celebrating my company's 25th anniversary.

The Rose Parade, true to its inception, is driven by a passion to promote and celebrate Pasadena, California, as a beautiful place to live and work. The parade was the brainchild of Pasadena's wealthy socialites who were in competition with their elite counterparts on the East Coast. As New Yorkers waited out forced hibernation and braved ice-coated streets, their Southern Californian counterparts were strolling in summer whites and playing golf under sun-drenched skies. The parade celebrated the gift of roses blooming in January. Eventually it grew in scope and popularity to become one of the most celebrated community events in the world. The Rose Bowl college football game was added in 1902 as a means of funding the parade. Every year, the streets of the parade route are lined with more than a million dedicated fans, while many more millions view it on television.

The Rose Parade is much more than pageantry and flowers. It's the crowning glory of more than 900 committed, community volunteers, who contribute vital support to every aspect of the production, donating countless hours and weekends to create this one spectacular event.

The Rose Parade Foundation, in turn, supports many local charities. The Rose Parade's commitment to collective social change, in this producer's eyes, underscores the true purpose of a successful event, which is not only to entertain, but also to affect lives, and in this case, change them as well.

I soon discovered that the experience of judging the parade proved to be a double-edged sword. Honored, as I was to participate in this labor of love, I was also daunted by the anxiety of being one of only three judges who would choose 24 winners from 46 floats.

The first of my three days on the job consisted of judge training and orientation. We had to rise pre-dawn every day finding ourselves up close and personal with an incredible array of floats of every shape and size, some still under construction. We were asked to view each and every float and ultimately choose 24 winners based on a variety of characteristics and categories. I don't mind telling you, I really wondered how it would all turn out. I found them all beautiful, each in their own way.

Official judging took place over 48 hours, as representatives introduced us to each float. In a word, the floats were spectacular.

OPPOSITE PAGE

Adventures in Space float at the 125th Pasadena Tournament of Roses® Parade

Awards ranged from the "Excellence in Presenting Parade Theme" to the "Most Effective Use and Display of Roses in Concept, Design and Presentation" and the "Most Comical and Amusing Entry" to the "Most Beautiful Float Built and Decorated by Volunteers from a Community or Organization". As impossible as I suspected it would be to choose winners, there were several floats that moved me on a deeply personal level and so, as always, I went with my instincts.

My colleagues and I voted individually, and after combined deliberation, the awards were handed out.

We, and all those who stood along the street or sat in the bleachers that day, experienced the same awe and wonder as these magnificent floral creations floated by, each one as beautiful and memorable as the one before it. The confetti, the music, the laughter, the marching bands and the horses were truly a living synchronized miracle, and believe me, it doesn't take an event producer to recognize the genius behind this mammoth effort.

I couldn't help wondering, as I watched the power of impassioned volunteers—people inspiring the world— what if we raised our sights beyond the scope of a parade? What if we all volunteered to change the world with as much passion and precision? Many of the individual floats did, in fact, draw vital public awareness to philanthropic issues.

This event business can be a whirlwind. The timelines, the details, the demands and the stress—they can wear you away like a pencil sharpener does a pencil. Every once in a while, you are privileged to be part of a monumental experience, working with people who really care about community; who care about something larger than their individual selves. Suddenly you're lifted, you're "floating", and once again you remember why you got into this business.

"Happiness does not come from doing easy work, but from the afterglow of satisfaction
that comes after the achievement of a difficult task that demanded our best."
—Theodore Isaac Rubin

OPPOSITE PAGE

Judging the spectacular
floats at the 125th Pasadena
Tournament of
Roses® Parade

272

The Best is Yet to Come?

TOMORROW AND TOMORROW

I knew this chapter would come. After some serious soul searching, I am able to articulate my perspective on the future. I'm not talking about the flying car or global warming future, as exciting or daunting as that future may be. I'm referring to the future that's in store for us, you and I, before our proverbial final bow.

It's said that as children, we live in the present, and that we are not aware of the march of time. In our productive years, time seems to scream by; at least it does for me. In our twilight years, we experience our lives once again very much in the here and now, since there may not be as many tomorrows ahead as there are yesterdays behind.

You know I have a big family. Nowadays that translates into many aunts, uncles and family friends who are quite elderly. I notice that the elderly spend much of their time reminiscing about their accomplishments, experiences and people along the way. They ask themselves, "How did I do? Did I live fully, and do what I set out to do?"

I find that the elderly treasure friends and loved ones who are in their lives today, right now. Whenever we call on long-retired relatives, especially when we bring our children along, the joy and appreciation that they radiate is palpable as soon as we arrive at their door. They live in the now.

I think the answer to the question about whether or not our lives were well-lived depends mostly on what we did with our lives every day, when "every day" was the present. It's really true, the past is past and tomorrow never comes.

Do I plan at some point to get back to the gym and eat more healthily, once I'm successful enough and have the time? No, I strive to live healthily every day. Do I plan, at some point, to finally come up for air, or turn off the big screen TV, or smell the proverbial roses? No—I love roses, both the literal and the metaphorical. Roses whither and die; they won't wait for me to start paying attention.

Have I marked a spot on the calendar indicating when I will miraculously start to act out of love and possibilities, rather than fear? No—it's important to me that my children experience me attempting to act from a place of love (the operative word being "attempting"), and learning from the times when I don't, because then I know they will strive to live more abundantly, generously, and peacefully.

OPPOSITE PAGE

Memorable moments

PAGE 276-277

A typical Cecchetto's Sunday

afternoon barbeque

It's certainly true that I spread the word about the importance of celebrating relationships and milestones right now, whether via producing an awards event, a bar mitzvah, a fundraiser for a hospital, or perhaps producing a film some day.

It seems to me, no matter how we look at it, that if we concentrate on manifesting the best "present" we can, with purpose and foresight, the future will take care of itself.

Is the best yet to come?

I believe the best is here today in this moment.

SEQUOIA
PRODUCTIONS

1988 Cheryl Cecchetto creates Sequoia Productions working from her dining room table with her part time assistant manning the typewriter and state-of-the-art fax machine.

2003
Los Angeles' fabled Park Plaza Hotel bursts back to life as we create a dazzling farewell celebration for one of the nation's all-time favorite sitcoms, *Friends*. The Rembrandts and Sheryl Crow perform to honor the cast and crew!

1989 OUR FLEDGING COMPANY IS HIRED BY THE ACADEMY OF MOTION PICTURE ARTS AND SCIENCES TO PRODUCE THE ACADEMY AWARDS® GOVERNORS BALL AT THE SHRINE AUDITORIUM.

Our team designs and creates the 1st Annual Entertainment Weekly, Pre-Emmy® Celebration in Los Angeles with a striking red, green and blue, "RGB" - colors of television theme.

1996

Our modest operation continues it's rapid expansion with "service" at the helm of our productions. A small, private gathering exacts the same commitment and attention to detail as a gala with a 1000 person guest list.

2002 The Academy of Motion Picture Arts and Sciences hosts Oscar's® long-awaited return to Hollywood, where we produce the first Ball at the Hollywood & Highland Grand Ballroom. In an unforgettable moment before guest arrival, the live koi centerpieces decide to make a swim for it!

Our team is featured in the luxury resource publication, Robb Report.

1998
OUR 3 person team moves from Cheryl's home into our first official office, where schedules are recorded on dry-erase boards and the fastest method of written communication is a quick trip to the post office.

2001
We close Hollywood Boulevard to create a Broadway-inspired stage for a star-studded show, complete with tuxedo-clad dancers and 500 pounds of biodegradable confetti, a spectacular opening for the new Hollywood & Highland Complex.

CHERYL ARRIVES AT HER HOMETOWN OF SUDBURY, CANADA, AND THE TEAM TRANSFORMS A LOCAL RECREATION CENTER'S CURLING RINK INTO A LUSH, HOLLYWOOD-INSPIRED BALLROOM.

Hosting 10,000 Angelinos and honoring 30 departments, we take on Cedars Sinai's 100th Anniversary Celebration.

2004 At the Pioneer Navigation Launch Event, our game-changing, red carpet "step & repeat" wall sets the typical "guest arrival" scenario on its ear, incorporating oversized plasma screens featuring motion graphics.

First published in 2014 by New Holland Publishers Pty Ltd
London • Sydney • Auckland

The Chandlery Unit 9, 50 Westminster Bridge Road London SE1 7QY United Kingdom
1/66 Gibbes Street Chatswood NSW 2067 Australia
218 Lake Road Northcote Auckland New Zealand

www.newhollandpublishers.com

A record of this book is held at the British Library and the National Library of Australia.

ISBN 9781742576039

Managing Director: Fiona Schultz
Project Editor: Angela Sutherland
Designer: Lorena Susak
Production Director: Olga Dementiev
Printer: Toppan Leefung Printing Ltd

10 9 8 7 6 5 4 3 2 1

Keep up with New Holland Publishers on Facebook
www.facebook.com/NewHollandPublishers

Keep up with Sequoia Productions on social media:
Facebook: SequoiaProductions
Twitter: @sequoiaevents
Instagram: sequoia_productions

US $35.00
UK £19.99

Epilogue

So here I am, working on the final edits of this book, absolutely exhausted. It's midnight. We returned to Los Angeles yesterday after producing two spectacular events, the Hard Hat Walk and Lights On Festival for the UCSF Medical Center at Mission Bay. It was a landmark occasion for UCSF and the city of San Francisco. The events concluded with *Modern Family's* Jesse Tyler Ferguson leading the countdown to a sensational light show finale.

Fast-forward to 24 hours later: * 16 hours to book deadline * resting my head on the table for 5-minute catnaps * Sequoia Productions team reading, spelling, pasting, collating * determined to power through * dedication is palpable * publishers not expecting this extra page at the 11th hour.

However, I would like to go on record regarding how honored we are to have produced these momentous events in San Francisco.

The past 25 years of supporting the commemoration of significant organizations and paying tribute to distinguished community landmarks is part of the history that defines Sequoia Productions. Day by day, event by event, year by year, we are fortunate to contribute to many incredible milestones. I hope you've enjoyed a glimpse into my world and that I have inspired your own *Passion to Create*!

People I Couldn't Do it Without

AND ALL THE ONES I FORGOT

Thank you to my mother and father for providing a childhood that was quite the "event" in itself, and to my sisters, who faithfully continue that tradition. Writing a book is a labor of love and a collaborative effort. Thank you to my son, Milan, for his unyielding love, to my daughter Mia, for her humor, talent and beauty, and to my husband Mike, for his patience and constant support. Argelia Luis, you run my home and save my life every day. How could I do what I do without you? Life would stop.

Olivia Yu: *Passion to Create* and Sequoia Productions Creative Director. Olivia, you deserve a special mention. You are the "O" in Sequoia Productions. Your tireless creativity knows no bounds. Your talented team, Hillary Ashen and Loma Gueno, are simply spectacular. Bert Hilkes: *Passion to Create* in-house Editor. Bert, without you, there would simply be no book. You have been my right hand and my left.

Thank you to the Sequoia Productions team for your patience and understanding when I was busy writing and conspicuously absent: Vice President Gary Levitt, Abe Andraos, Lauren Johnson Ashamalla, Samantha Bass, Michelle Chan, Theresa Clayton Taylor, Chelsea Cowley, Annie De Vera, Erlinda dela Cruz, Mandy Dials, Eleanor Dizon, Andrea Drake Brooks, Heather Forster, Meghan Gudelsky, Alex Kalognomos, Matt Kenney, Jessica Montri, Karen Rosolowski, Tara Schroetter, Jason Singer, and Caitlin Strittmatter. Thank you to Chari Ludwin for your inspiration! Thank you to Lesley Kyle-Wilson, Alyse Sobel, and Victoria Kemsley.

A special thank you to the artists Irma Hardjamakusumah, Keith Greco, Rohit Fernandez and Justin Knause for your inspired renderings and incredible talent.

A special thank you to Cheryl Boone Isaacs, Dawn Hudson, Christina Kounelias, Teni Melidonian, and Natalie Kojen of the Academy of Motion Picture Arts and Sciences, and to Emily Benedict for suggesting our beautiful cover photograph. A special thank you to Bruce Rosenblum, Maury McIntyre, Heather Cochran, and Laurel Whitcomb from the Television Academy. Thank you Steve Mersereau! A big thank you to G'DAY USA and Beaulieu Vineyards for your support. Thank you to my delightful manager, Steve McArthur at The Buzz Group, and to the ever patient Fiona Schultz at New Holland Publishers.

On behalf of Sequoia Productions, thank you to all of my valued clients, and all of their staff. To all of my cherished technicians, artisans and the staff who have worked as part of the Sequoia Productions team; where would our projects be without you? Thank you to dress designer Ali Rahimi, and John Barle at Mon Atelier, to Jeweler Michael O'Connor, and to clothing stylists Connie and David Oliver.

To my dear friends and family, I celebrate you all. Without listening, sharing and creating with all of you throughout the days and years, I would have never learned to celebrate life, to fight, to fish, to cook, to eat, to yell, to listen, to lose, to win, to play, to sing and to love. I am forever grateful.

OPPOSITE PAGE

Plating first course at 57th
Primetime Emmys®
Governors Ball

Nadine Froger Photography

282

CHAPTER 10

I'd Like to Thank

My Sisters' Blueberry Pie

INGREDIENTS

Crust

1 egg

1 tablespoon white vinegar

Water

5 cups (1¼ lb/565 g) all-purpose (plain) flour,
   plus extra for dusting

1 teaspoon baking powder

½ teaspoon salt

4 teaspoons brown sugar

1 lb (450 g) solid vegetable shortening

Filling

4–5 cups (1–1¼ lb/450–565 g) fresh or frozen blueberries

½ cup (4 oz/115 g) granulated (white) sugar, plus extra for
   dusting

2 tablespoons all-purpose (plain) flour

1 tablespoon lemon juice

MAKES 2 X 9 IN. (23 CM) PIES

METHOD

For the crust

1. In a measuring cup mix together the egg and vinegar.
   Add enough water to measure ¾ cup (6 fl oz/175 ml).
2. Put the flour, baking powder, salt and brown sugar in a bowl, cut in the shortening with two knives (or use your fingertips) until large breadcrumbs form. Add the liquid a little at a time using just enough until the mixture can be kneaded into a ball. Divide into equal portions.
3. Roll out one portion on a lightly floured surface to a 10 in. (25 cm) round and fit into a 9 in (23 cm) pie dish, leaving overhang. Repeat to line a second pie dish.

For the filling

1. Preheat the oven to 425°F/220°C.
2. Combine all filling ingredients in a bowl and mix well.
   Divide evenly between the pastry cases.
3. Roll out each remaining dough portion on a floured surface, one at a time. Cut each into strips and arrange in a lattice over each pie filling. Crimp the edges.
4. Bake for 15 minutes. Reduce the oven temperature to 350°F/180°C and continue baking for another 30 minutes, or until golden brown and the blueberries are bubbling. Add foil around the crust edges during baking if they begin to over-brown).
5. Sprinkle the tops with a little sugar. Place under the broiler (grill) quickly to brown, if desired.